PSYCHO BUSTERS

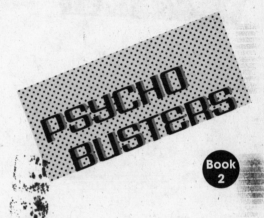

Book 2

Illustrations by Rando Ayamine
Translated by Katy Bridges

BALLANTINE BOOKS NEW YORK

PSYCHO BUSTERS

THE NOVEL

YUYA AOKI

A Del Rey Manga/Kodansha Trade Paperback Original

Published in the United States by Del Rey Books, an imprint of The Random House Publishing Group, a division of Random House, Inc., New York.

DEL REY is a registered trademark and the Del Rey colophon is a trademark of Random House, Inc.

Publication rights arranged through Kodansha Ltd.

First published in Japan in 2004 by Kodansha Ltd., Tokyo, as *Saikobasutaazu 2*.

Library of Congress Cataloging-in-Publication Data
Aoki, Yuya.
(Saiko basutazu. English)
Psycho busters : the novel / Yuya Aoki ; illustrations by Rando Ayamine ; translated by Katy Bridges.
    p. cm.
ISBN-13: 978-0-345-50061-8 (v. 2 : pbk.)
I. Ayamine, Rando. II. Bridges, Katy. III. Title.
PL867.5.O43S25 2008
895.6'36—dc22   2007043846

Printed in the United States of America

www.delreymanga.com

9 8 7 6 5 4 3 2 1

Translator/adapter: Katy Bridges
Cover illustration: Rando Ayamine
Text design: Karin Batten

CONTENTS

ILLUSTRATIONS

PSYCHO BUSTERS

Book 2

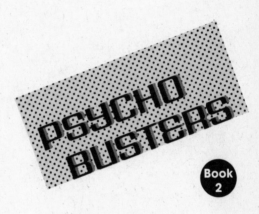

Mamoru Kamichika, a young detective in the Juvenile Division of the police, didn't know what to do. Whenever the department had a young girl in custody, it was always the youthful and likable Kamichika who was tasked with interrogating her.

It was really a job for a policewoman. He had asked his boss to hire one, but to no avail. His boss only said, "A nice guy like you gets the girls to let their guard down."

As for Kamichika, he had a girlfriend, so he was neither happy with nor grateful for this role, but even so, the experience was beginning to give him greater confidence in himself.

This time, however, he wasn't having any luck. The girl was like an empty shell. They were in the interrogation room, which was completely bare save for a table and chair. She hadn't uttered a word in two hours, but just sat there with her head hanging down, as if in shame. No matter how he spoke to her or what he said, she did not respond.

They had quickly deduced her identity from her personal effects. She was the student, a ninth grader at a junior high school in the city, for whom they'd been asked to search one week ago. After school, she'd gone to an extracurricular study center—but never come home.

She was still wearing the school uniform—the midi blouse and blue pleated skirt—that she'd been wearing at the time of her disappearance. But its condition was too good to have been worn for a whole week. The skirt was unwrinkled, and the sleeves and the collar were completely unsoiled. Her hair was also neat.

The girl's parents were divorced, and she lived with her mother, a busy fashion magazine editor. She didn't get along with her mother, so the girl had tried to run away from home several times. This time was no different. The police doubted the seriousness of the incident and had not put much effort into their search. She had been found earlier that evening, at seven p.m. About four hours ago.

Headquarters had immediately contacted her mother, who was on a business trip; it seemed she wouldn't be able to pick up her daughter until late that night. What did it mean that her mother not only kept working while her daughter was missing, *but went on a business trip*? Kamichika felt he understood why this girl wanted to run away.

She had been discovered in a playground in a deserted residential area, surrounded by five teenaged boys. All the boys were notorious delinquents from the area, and they had probably brought the girl there with the intention of doing something bad to her—or so the policeman who discovered her had said. But they had not achieved their goal. On the contrary, judging from her appearance, they had not even laid a finger on her.

In fact, the five punks were found near the girl, who was in a daze. All five were unconscious and covered in blood. According to the officer who had discovered them, it was as if they'd been attacked by a gorilla. One had a shattered leg; another had foam coming from his mouth, his body twisted like a rag; still another had gone into convulsions. An ambulance was summoned immediately and the girl taken into protective custody.

It was soon apparent that the situation was a serious one. Kamichika was called from the Juvenile Division, and now he was expected to interrogate a girl who refused to speak.

"Please, won't you say something?" Kamichika threw out the words he'd repeated dozens of times.

Actually, Kamichika had his own suspicions about her disappearance. In the last two weeks, seventeen boys and girls had disappeared. And, like the girl, each had left for cram-school and never returned home. They had all had problems at home, so his boss interpreted the unusual number of runaways as mere coincidence, but Kamichika didn't agree. Instead, he had an awful feeling that something terrible was about to happen here in this peaceful community.

Because she was the first of the runaways they'd taken into protective custody, he was hoping to get some information out of her that could possibly hint at what had happened to the others. "What happened? How did those boys end up covered with blood? Could you think about it? None of them have regained consciousness yet. You're the only one I can ask."

Slowly she moved her eyes to Kamichika. It was the first time she'd responded in the two hours they'd sat facing each other. *Good, she's finally going to open up,* Kamichika thought.

His confidence growing, Kamichika went on to his main question: "Have you calmed down a bit? Good, then I'll tell you what I think happened. If it's close to what you know, then nod. All right? In early evening, those five boys called out to you, and they brought you to that park. Just as things were starting to get bad, some-one else came . . . probably not alone, maybe a few peo-ple all together, and they were big guys who knew karate or something, and then they started a fight over you with the first five guys and—"

She opened her mouth. "It wasn't like that."

"Huh?" said Kamichika. Although this was what he'd hoped for, he was as stunned as if he'd been slapped. "What wasn't like that? Could you please give me details? Why did something so terrible happen—"

"I did it." She smiled. It was a smile of triumph.

"*You* did? Ha ha, surely not. Whatever the circum-stances, there were five of them and one of you. Or are you a black belt in karate? No, even if you were, I think it would be hard even for a karate champion to inflict such major damage."

"You don't have to believe me. I have amazing pow-ers. Amazing powers . . ." As she murmured this, the girl's eyes rolled back in her head, and she began to shake as if feverish.

"H-hey, are you all right?" Kamichika grabbed her shoulders.

She glared at Kamichika with bloodshot eyes. "Let go!" she shrieked.

Then it happened.

A pain like an electric shock ran through both of Kamichika's hands. Next, he was flung against the wall behind him by something that felt like a blast of air pres-sure.

"Guah!" What Kamichika saw as he groaned and slid down the wall to the floor was the shaking form of the girl emitting a death scream.

"He-hey, are you . . ." Heroically quelching the pain in his back, Kamichika went toward the girl.

He coughed so hard he was almost unable to breathe.

"A-are you all right? Hey . . ." he coughed. His head swam.

Abruptly the girl stopped screaming. She smiled through her tears. And then she murmured clearly:

"Kakeru Hase."

Right after that, her head turned dark red, began to swell, and exploded, making a noise like a watermelon breaking.

Kamichika ran out of the interview room as blood rained down all around him.

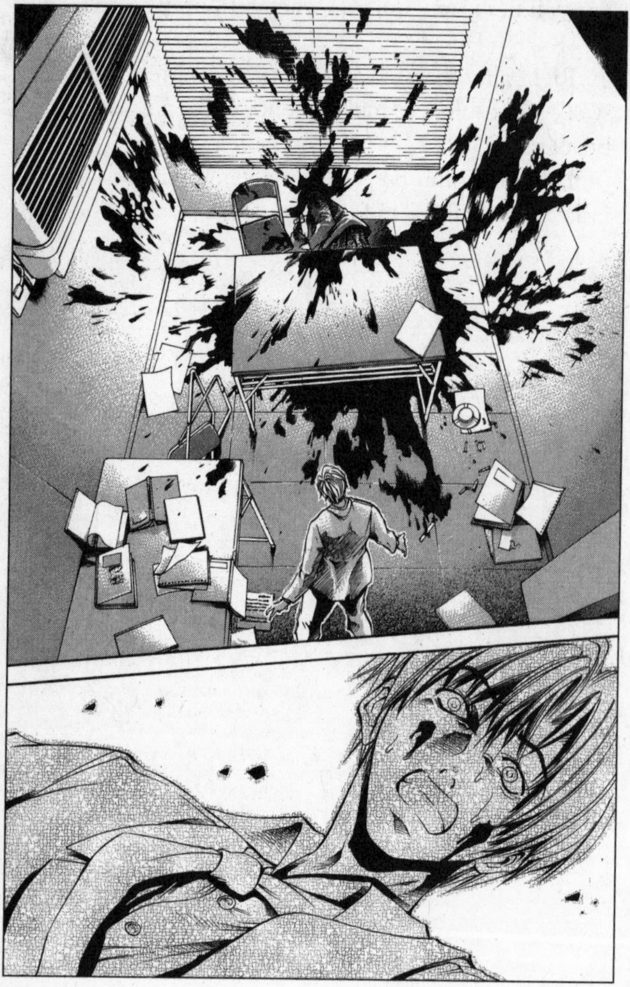

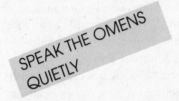

CHAPTER 1

SPEAK THE OMENS QUIETLY

"Okay, I'm going to school!" I took the last bite of my sandwich as I put on my blazer.

"Wait just a minute, Kakeru!" Mother frowned. "There's no need to leave in such a hurry, is there? And you're not in any school clubs . . ."

"She's right, Kakeru. You've been kind of weird lately. You used to drink coffee, watch TV, and browse the newspaper mindlessly until the last possible minute," said the younger of my older sisters.

The oldest of my sisters was in college, and had just woken up. She made no move to pick up her breakfast sandwich as she stared vacuously at the TV news.

"I have something I have to do at school. With friends," I said.

It was true. But I couldn't talk in front of my family about who those friends were and what we were going to do. It wasn't something that could be explained in a few words, and there was a chance that as soon as I'd finished explaining they'd take me to the hospital.

"What is it you have to do? Lately, you've been doing

this every morning, and still you get home from school really late. You're not doing anything you shouldn't, are you?"

"Really, Mom, it's okay. I wouldn't do anything like that. Okay, see ya!" I slipped on my shoes and dashed out of the house. It would not have been good if she had asked me to go into any detail and I'd given it all away.

My friends had already come inside the door to get me. *Ready to go, Kakeru?* Ayano asked with a smile, her face literally transparent. Ayano Fujimura—a girl with the ability to psychically project herself outside her body who had transferred into my class.

Her semitransparent astral body was clad, modestly and appropriately, in a school uniform. When I had first met her a month ago, she had appeared before me naked, which had made our first meeting in the real world a little awkward.

But her mastery over her ability had since grown, and now she could do several things with her talent. One of them was creating a "physical body" that could wear clothes. Another was to project herself into animals and manipulate them.

It's okay. Shall we go, Ayano? I didn't use my voice, but gave a small nod of assent to convey my thought to Ayano.

Having this kind of conversation via telepathy, without having to take her ethereal body into mine, was another of Ayano's new skills.

Great, everyone's waiting outside.

By "everyone," Ayano meant all the other psychics who had escaped the mysterious Greenhouse, a facility in which psychics with supernatural powers were trained.

"Bye! I'm leaving!" I turned back to my mom and sisters, who had poked their heads out of the dining room, and waved as I opened the door.

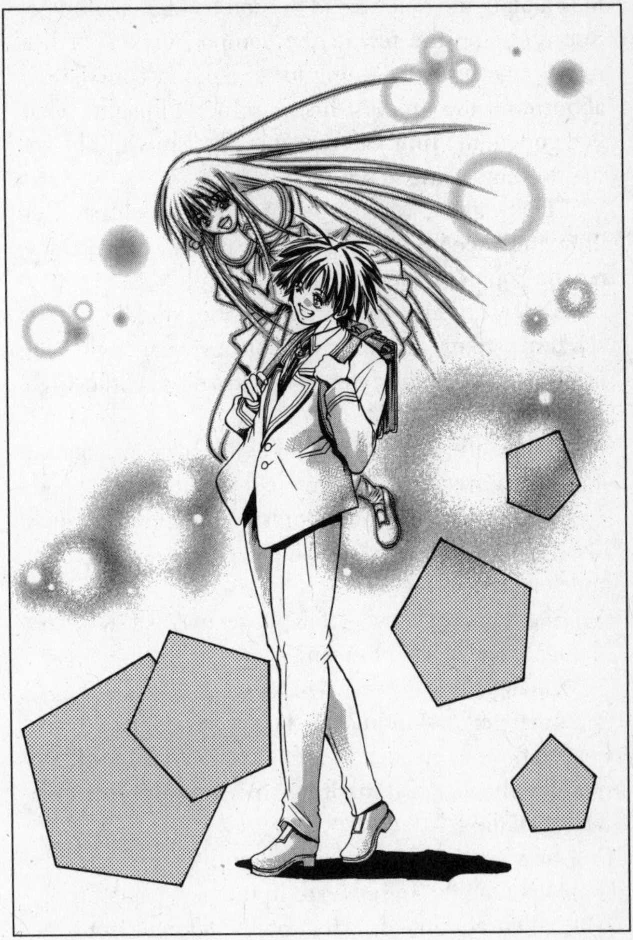

Then I ran down the several concrete stairs double-time to where my friends were.

"Strange, isn't it?" Kakeru's mother, Kumiko Hase, took a bit of the onion salad her son had left behind before dumping the rest in the compost basket. "Till a month ago he hated going to school and complained about it all the time. At first, I couldn't imagine what had gotten into him, but now it really seems as if he actually enjoys going to school."

"That's great, Mom," said Suzue, the eldest. Her drowsiness seemed to have finally passed, because she reached out for a sandwich.

"I'm worried," said Hanae, the middle child. "Kakeru's going into high school next year, right? It's not going to be my fault if he doesn't get into high school!"

"It'll be all right, Hanae. I'll be his tutor and pound it into him over the summer. He'll pass for sure."

"Well, aren't *you* the optimist! You know what he's like—gutless! He hated studying to get into junior high, and you know it."

"Yeah, but y'know, lately it seems like Kakeru's changed. Know what I mean?"

"Changed?"

"Changed, as in maybe he's a little more level-headed now. Ever since we went to Hawaii without him he's somehow . . . I think it was living on his own for a week that did it."

"No way. You're imagining things," said Hanae, absently looking through the ads in the newspaper on the table, then continued, "He's totally different from me and Suzue. He's like Dad. Normally guys like them never get ahead in the world if you just leave them be."

"My goodness, Hanae, what a thing to say!" rebuked

Kumiko. "Don't say bad things about your father. After all, who do you think helped raise you all these years?"

"Yes, Mother."

"I didn't. It was Hanae."

"Oh, as if you don't say the same stuff when we're alone!"

"Tattletale!"

"That's enough, you two. Anyway, your father is off working down in Kyushu without his family in order to support the whole family. Remember that."

"Yes, Mother."

Hanae gave a halfhearted answer as she cruised through the ads in the newspaper. Her hand stopped. "Oh, here's that Supplemental Education center everyone's talking about. Wow, they're taking on new students. Have you heard about it, Mom?"

"The Supplemental Education center? What about it?"

"It's getting quite a reputation around here. The tutoring center that just opened up in front of the train station. They say they can move your class standing up between five to ten places in just two weeks."

"Ridiculous. Who could believe outlandish claims like that?"

"But Mom, it is really amazing. My friend's little brother goes to the same junior high school that Kakeru does, and he says the kids there take the mock standardized college entrance test at a much bigger study center that's a national chain, and they always come out in the top percentile. And then as soon as he started going to that tutoring center himself, it was unbelievable how much his grades improved. So, Mom, I thought, what about enrolling Kakeru there . . ."

"That sounds suspicious to me. Something smells."

So saying, Suzue returned her half-eaten sandwich to her plate.

"What do you mean, 'something smells'?" asked Hanae.

"It happens a lot these days. I mean it sounds like one of those weird cults or something."

"Ah ha ha, you're exaggerating, Suzue. It's only a tutoring center."

"Haven't you heard, Suzue? Recently a lot of junior high students have been disappearing."

"No, I didn't know. I haven't heard a thing about it."

"Well, what they all have in common is that they were all going to a new tutoring center that just opened up. The police are watching it. What if that's the one you're talking about?"

"Now sis! Where'd you hear that? Oh, that detective guy, right?"

"Would you stop calling him that? Call him Mr. Kamichika, or Mamoru or something like that, because he may end up becoming your brother-in-law someday."

"Whoa, have you guys already gotten that far? Knock it off, wives of police detectives are never happy. On all those TV shows they always seem so miserable."

"Lay off. And don't tell Kakeru, because he doesn't know my boyfriend's a police detective."

"All *right*, already."

"Going back to what we were just talking about, it seems that all the kids who disappeared had problems at home, and it looks like they're thinking they just ran away. There sure will be a big fuss if it's a cult."

"Eeuw, stop telling stories like that! Geez. I won't be able to go out alone at night!"

"All right, both of you, finish your breakfast and get

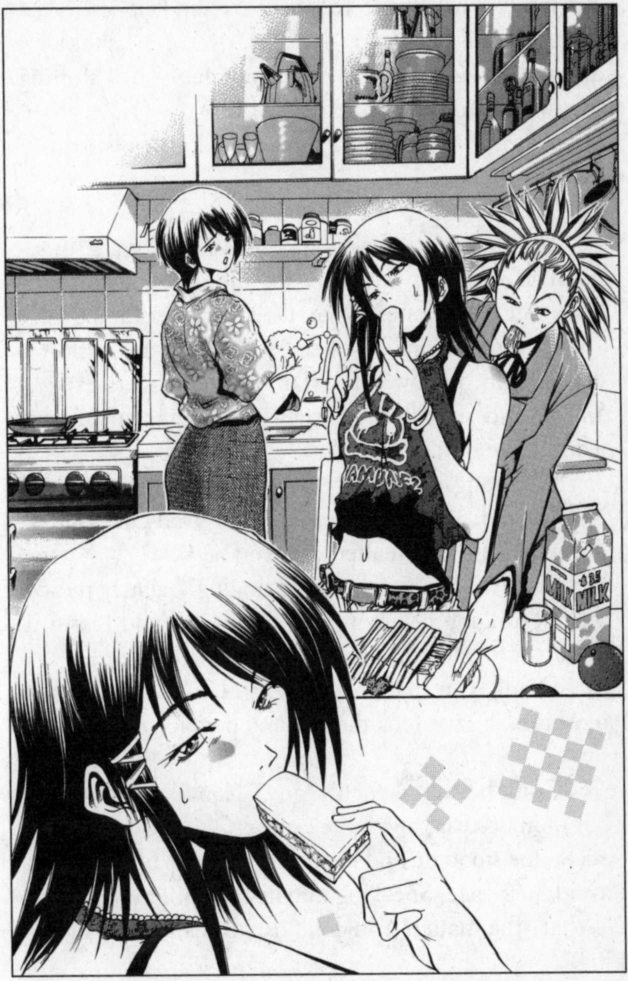
MILK
MILK

to school," said Kumiko, and began washing dishes to hurry them up.

As if the sound of running water was a signal, the two sisters quickly ate the rest of their sandwiches. "And Suzue," said Kumiko, looking over her shoulder, amazed at how quickly her daughters were stuffing sandwiches into their mouths, "if you are serious about marrying Mr. Kamichika, you should at least learn to cook a little."

"Yes, Mom."

"Your father and I won't oppose you marrying some-one you're in love with, but the life of a police detective's wife is not an easy one. Do you understand that?"

"It's okay, Mom. I've been seeing him for almost a year already. I know better than you do what to expect. You've only ever been married to a businessman who works in an office."

"Who taught you to speak that way?"

"You did, of course, Mom. I mean, Dad's the kind of guy who smiles no matter what you say . . ."

"Sis, is that your cell phone ringing?" Hanae pulled out the ringing cell from her sister's bag and tossed it to her.

"Thank you. Hello? Oh, hi! Uh . . . yeah, good morning." Suzue took the call and her face relaxed in a smile.

"Gotta be that detective guy," Hanae whispered in her mother's ear.

Suzue stood up and headed toward the front door to avoid their gaze. Speaking into her cell phone, she said, "What's the matter? You don't usually call in the morning."

"Suzue, there's something I want to ask you about," said Kamichika.

"To ask me?"

"Uh huh. It's about your little brother Kakeru . . ."

At the unexpected mention of her brother's name, Suzue decided to joke. "Oh, come on, did he do something bad?"

"I don't know. But if I'm right, he's a key witness in a case."

"Huh?" At this statement, so far removed from what she expected to hear from her boyfriend, Suzue nearly dropped her cell phone.

The building looked like a cake box abandoned in the middle of the forest.

It had almost no windows, and no details on the outside walls attracted attention. A gigantic concrete cube painted white. Officially registered as an agricultural experiment station, this building was called the Greenhouse.

A morning breeze had cleared the woods of mist. When the big building reared up in front of them, the five government agents could not help but touch the weapons they carried to make sure they were there.

That's how strange a scene it was.

It was two weeks ago that Yugo Shikishima, of a Special Services branch of the National Police Agency, and five people who worked under him, had been ordered to investigate this mysterious building. Their task was to verify what was really going on inside this strange building on an immense private estate.

That had been the only explanation they'd been given. Who was their enemy? What was going on in there? Was it an ordinary crime, or was it terrorism? Shikishima had asked his superior these things many times but hadn't obtained any answers.

He was frankly perplexed. It was natural that a

branch of the Secret Service, whose existence itself was unknown by the public, would be mobilized to do things in secret, but as one might expect, he had no experience with going on missions on which he had been given so little information. However, if he wasn't mistaken, what was going on in that cake box wasn't more than simple "illegal activity."

They'd walked for half a day through the forest, which was humid from the abundant ferns. By the time they had arrived at their destination, guided by the map in his handheld navigation device, the sun was rising.

According to the pictures taken by helicopter, the top of the building was a heliport, and it looked like supplies and people were being transported in and out by helicopter. The permit for this building licensed it as a private-sector agricultural experiment station, but what kind of fruits and vegetables could they be researching in this peculiar building, in this inconvenient location that could only be reached by helicopter . . . and that was also inaccessible to sunlight?

Keeping a sharp lookout, he approached the only entrance that could be confirmed from the outside, in an inconspicuous corner.

The security cameras installed here and there on the walls were activated by infrared sensors, and they followed every move Shikishima and the others made.

"Everyone be on the lookout. We could find ourselves under fire," said Shikishima. He took out his own pistol and got ready.

Then it happened.

There was a metallic clang. The handle of the gigantic door turned from the inside, and with a creak that hurt his ears, the door opened. Shikishima's breath caught in his throat. He pointed the mouth of his gun toward the darkness inside the building.

"Ahhh!" came a girl's voice.

Intuitively concluding from the voice that there was no attack, the government agents lowered their weapons.

There stood a girl in white. She was fair-skinned and dewy-eyed, with long dark hair falling down her back. And, incredibly beautiful.

Bobbing his head in regret to pointing his gun at such a woman, he said "E-excuse me! My na . . . my name is Shikishima. Uh, I'm an inspector. I was sent by a secret branch of the police . . ."

One of the team covering his back looked at Shikishima and gave a wry grin. Even Shikishima, nicknamed the Drill Sergeant, turned to mush in front of a beautiful woman.

"Oh, no," she smiled, shaking her head. "The security cameras showed me that it was someone to do with the police, and still I screamed, so I'm the one who should be apologizing. Please come in. I can't imagine what might have brought you here . . ." She spoke with deep courtesy.

Although confused and betrayed by their expectations, the five inspectors, including Shikishima, changed their minds about staying on their guard and walked into the building.

Contrary to its bleak outward appearance, the "cake box" was surprisingly bright and cheerful on the inside. From the outside, it seemed to have few windows, but once inside, a giant skylight was visible, through which such an abundance of sunlight was pouring that it no longer seemed they were in the middle of a forest. Also, powerful artificial lights overlooked a huge space in which plants grew abundantly. The building was every inch an agricultural testing center.

Many agricultural workers hummed happily as they worked, the expressions on their faces not revealing even the slightest shadow of criminality. When any one of them spotted Shikishima and the others, he smiled and said hello. As Shikishima and his men stood there dripping in military accoutrements, Shikishima could only feel he'd made himself and his men look like fools.

A pleasant temperature and level humidity for plants and people were maintained in the open hallwaylike space. The plants were heavily laden with gigantic red, yellow, and brilliant orange fruit; the vegetables with luxuriant healthy leaves. One of the workers plucked a rare southern fruit and offered it to Shikishima.

"Oh! Uh, no thanks. I'm on duty."

Thus politely refused, the agricultural worker bowed his head in apology, then, still smiling, bit into the fruit himself.

"It looks delicious," one of Shikishima's team whispered in his ear. "Could we ask for one to take home as a souvenir?"

"Don't be stupid," replied Shikishima.

But he started to salivate as he realized how hungry he was.

"Everyone looks happy, don't they," said the woman guiding them. "You may find it strange to have an agricultural testing laboratory this deep in the mountains, but unless we are isolated, there are some things we cannot do."

"Is that why this is here?" Shikishima couldn't think of what could only be done someplace so isolated, except for something illegal.

"We are testing whether crops are affected by the happiness and affection of the people raising them. So we cannot conduct this experiment in a place subject to the hustle and bustle of the city, where the plants may be disturbed by the negative vibes of city dwellers."

"Interesting" was Shikishima's only response.

What an absolutely crazy experiment. But strangely, Shikishima felt himself being persuaded by both her smiling face and the atmosphere of happiness that even he could feel. "Well, I see. This building really is an agricultural testing center, just like its permit said it is. But as a routine precaution, we'll need to examine what agricultural products are being grown here. I'm sorry about this, but we've come here on official business."

"Certainly, be my guest. Stay as long as you like," she said, giving them a smile more dazzling than the riotously blooming fruit blossoms.

After searching the building for over an hour, the investigators for the Special Service branch of the National Police Agency left the Greenhouse.

"They were easy enough to get rid of," she said, looking at the image of herself reflected in the large mirror on the wall next to the door. "Humph. Men that age will always fall for a pretty face." She spat at herself in the mirror, scoffing at her reflection.

Then it happened.

The supple hair down her back, the dewy eyes, and the long-limbed slender body were crushed like clay. At the same time, the surrounding scenery twisted, and what appeared in its place was something completely different.

What the inspectors had seen was an illusion—no, something more incomprehensible, something that was only inside their heads. What had seemed to be a luxuriant indoor farm was simply the inside of a bleak concrete box without even a single houseplant in sight. A hall lined with fluorescent lights that emitted unnatural light. Cold linoleum floors. And red emergency lights that spread their glare like a scar across the walls. What had seemed to be a hall burgeoning with fruits and vegetables was instead a gloomy laboratory.

Of course, there were no windows in the ceiling. Instead of plants, there were lines of unidentified machines, the computer displays projecting wallpaper images. The background images were all the same, sweeping agricultural vistas of green. Quite possibly intended ironically.

And the "woman" who had met the intruders became a girl of fourteen about whom there was still an air of childishness. Her sleek, white outfit transformed into black jeans and a black long-sleeved T-shirt. Her hair, so like a Japanese doll's, did not quite reach her shoulders. And the eyes, formerly big enough to fall into, were once again long, sharp slits.

"Splendid, Maya." Arata Ikushima clapped his hands together exaggeratedly as he appeared. "Sending telepathic images to five opponents at once is exceptional progress. Last month it was all you could do to take on one opponent at a time."

Ikushima was one of three people in charge of orchestrating the instructors, called Farmers, who trained the psychics at the Greenhouse. Maya and the other psychics were, after all, the real carrots and the cabbage.

Giving a derisive snort, Maya said, "Isn't it because you used all those pesticides? That's why we've grown up. . . . It's still nice though."

"Yes, it's nice. Very. How many opponents can you project into at the same time now, Maya?"

"I'll show stuff to you and everybody here, if you want. But still, it disgusts me that they saw me in the form of a showy woman like that."

The images created by the telepathy she sent to others were images she herself drew in her own brain. So it was natural she also saw them herself. Strong autosuggestions such as these were transmitted to others as telepathy.

"What about giving me medicine? I have to get back to 'work,' so I'll need a lot."

What Maya called "medicine" was a drug that was developed to cultivate latent psychic powers. Although with someone like Maya, whose powers had already manifested completely, it was almost useless.

"All right. But be sure you don't take too much, okay?" Ikushima took a case containing tablets out of his pocket and tossed it to Maya.

"Thank you." Maya looked as if she might drool as she opened the case, picked up a pill, and popped it into her mouth.

She gave a laugh. "Well now, time to be on my way. I'm not hanging around in this dreary concrete box any more than I have to." Maya thrust her hand in her pocket and started walking. Suddenly a dark, insubstantial human shape that almost simultaneously took the form of a teenage boy appeared before her.

Teleportation, or instantaneous movement between places via psychic power.

"Oh, Sho, it's you. Could you send me up to the heliport?"

"If I'm gonna do that, why not send you all the way to where you're working? It's a hundred times easier than going by helicopter."

Maya giggled again. "Well, okay then," she said, and extended her hand.

"Hold on tight, okay?" No sooner were the words out of his mouth than the two of them disappeared like an apparition. Ikushima furtively snickered to himself, gasping at the breathtaking ability of the two psychic monsters.

The two had made progress beyond imagining. In just the space of one month, their abilities had improved a thousand times over.

Losing Takemaru, the psychokineticist, with his ready firepower had been a bitter blow, but even allowing for his loss, their total combat power had increased. Happily, the two of them had gotten it into their minds that their new growth was due to the newly developed drug. So, mouths watering, they dosed themselves with placebos. With pills that were merely lumps of vitamins and minerals.

Ikushima played with one in his palm. He would be able to control those monsters as long as they had that impression.

"So . . . a 'Category Zero,'" he said without thinking, and hurriedly looked around to make sure no one had heard him. The other Farmers must not know that the surprising progress they had made was due to meeting a Category Zero.

Other than Ikushima, the other Farmers were, as always, assiduous in conducting psychic training, which required the use of dangerous medications and machines. Even though recently the damage from the cruel treatments they'd been inflicting on their subjects—dosing them with electromagnetic waves and harmful drugs—was beginning to show.

"It looks like you got rid of them nicely, Ikushima." Udoh Karaki, the director of the Greenhouse, approached him, his twin female secretaries in tow.

Since the incident one month before, Karaki had been in some trouble for his cruel experiments. And soon enough, his misdeeds were sure to come to the attention of Masquerade, the Frontier Committee—the mysterious group who funded the Greenhouse project. So it wouldn't be long before the Karaki reign was over. However . . .

"Yes," said Ikushima, "but there's nothing to worry about. Times like this are why we have our psychics."

"Humph. You talk like it's your own achievement," said Karaki as he headed for the office, without stopping before Ikushima.

The twin secretaries, looking for all the world like a pair of obedient collie dogs, tossed condescending smiles at Ikushima as they passed.

Even this little exchange expressed keenly that Karaki intended to get rid of Ikushima in the near future. Cold sweat appeared on Ikushima's brow. His only option was to create an insurrection. It was his only road to survival.

To accomplish this, the first thing he needed to do was awaken that Category Zero. The means was already at his disposal. He could use Karaki's blunder to kill two birds with one stone.

"You'll see, Karaki . . ." Ikushima muttered as he crushed the pill in the palm of his hand.

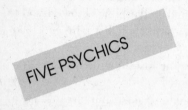

CHAPTER 2

FIVE PSYCHICS

"Hey, you, what're you thinking! Come off it!" said Teenage Boy A.

Uh, "Teenage Boy A" is hard to understand. Let's at least call him something generic, like Taro. He was in ninth grade, the same as me, and I knew he was just another low-level punk in a group of dropout types, but no matter how many times I heard his name, I could never remember what it was.

I mean, like everybody in his crowd, he's got dyed brown hair, an out-of-style blazer with an embroidered lining, and he tops off this look with big baggy pants with shiny knees that look like they're about to fall right off his backside. A punk from the sticks is still from the sticks.

One of my friends is also a delinquent, but he's from Yokohama and has somewhat more refined taste. The punks from my school look like characters in a *tsuppari* (although no one calls juvenile delinquents *tsuppari* anymore) manga.

But of course, I couldn't *actually* say that out loud.

There were five of them and just one of me. And it's not like I'm tall, can do karate, or have a surefire secret weapon or anything. Well, okay, that I *did* have.

I keep a paralyzer in a hidden pocket in the lining of my blazer. It's a super-small stun gun. But you can't go pulling something like that on a bunch of school punks.

Normally I would have thought I was destined to get beaten to a bloody pulp—but I wasn't afraid one bit.

And the reason I wasn't afraid was because Ayano was inside me right now.

It's all right, I just summoned Jôi and Kaito, she said to encourage me.

It had been a month since Ayano had been admitted to Kikyo ga Oka Junior High, the school I went to. And before even a week had passed, she had attracted the interest of every boy in the school. Ayano was such a megaton beauty that it made you wonder what she was even doing in a backwood school like this.

The reason why a regular guy like me, or, as those punks would put it, a boring little geek like me who was like the invisible man who you never knew was there, had actually attracted enough notice to warrant getting beaten up by a group of punks like this actually also lay with Ayano.

Ayano and I were close friends, and these guys couldn't stand to see us having any fun. Ayano and I sat next to each other in class. This was also just by chance, but it was why these guys thought we were good friends. This was actually a mistake.

We were, along with Jôi Toma and Kaito Himuro from the next class, and a second generation immigrant from China in the seventh grade named Xiao Long Baim, *comrades* who had survived a dangerous psychic battle.

"Hey, you? Ya listenin' ta me?" Taro (not his real name) grabbed me by the collar threateningly.

His nostrils were huge, *and* there was hair sticking out of them.

"Uh . . . um, I . . ."

Take it easy, Kakeru. Jôi and the others will be here soon. Your psychokinesis is dangerous. You're strong enough to destroy an entire gymnasium. And if things didn't go well, you could kill this guy, and then our secret might be discovered.

Even taking it easy, psychokinesis—the power to move things and even destroy them with your mind— was not something I had even a touch of.

No way could I stop these juvenile delinquents.

But Ayano was inside me. If I thought about my lack of psychokinesis, then Ayano would find out the truth, so I did my best not to give in to the fear. So this is what I thought.

Humph.

If I used psychokinesis on you guys, I could make mincemeat out of you in two seconds. I warn you, my patience has limits. You have as long as it takes for me to count to five . . . well, no ten, to get your hands off me.

I'll count as slowly as I can.

One—

Two—

Three—

Fou——r

Fi——ve . . .

"Hey! Say something!"

Then the boy—Taro—bared his teeth threateningly, like a chimpanzee, and got ready to give me a head butt, which these guys called a "Cho-pan."

Uh oh!

I shut my eyes as Taro moved his head back a little to give the blow more force, but the momentum carried him over backward and he fell—*splat*—on the ground.

"Huh? What?"

He fell over backward and kept striking the back of his head on the concrete, *thunk, thunk, thunk*.

An out-of-body projection!

"Ow, that hurts! Ow! S-somebody help . . . !"

But the punks surrounding me were panicking.

"What are you doing? Hey!" They jumped on Taro, like you'd jump on a horse, to hold him down, to stop him from torturing himself.

"Hey, you! What did you do?" Jiro (another generic name for another generic punk), who was part of the main group, came at me with fists flying.

"Wait" came a low voice, as Jiro's arms were caught behind him.

"Huh!?"

He turned around and promptly got smacked with a head butt to the face.

Jiro sank down to his knees without a sound, and crouched, blood dripping from his nose.

"Whaddya want with my friend?" Wiping blood that had come from Jiro's nose from his forehead, Kaito Himuro gave the surrounding punks a pointed look.

In the nick of time.

Saved.

This was the delinquent from Yokohama who I knew.

His shirt was unbuttoned, exposing his chest, and he'd altered his blazer so that his lapels were skinnier than the other guys'. His pants were just a little wider, and the cuffs were maybe just a little narrower. He was tall, so this look worked on him.

It was still only one month since he and Jôi, who was as handsome as a male model, had been admitted to the school, but they were already like local stars to the girl who sat next to me in class.

"Hey, Himuro! You gonna fight, or what? C'mon!" Contrary to their words, the punks were backing away. "Our leader is Jun Todoroki. You still want to pick a fight with us? Huh?!"

Jun Todoroki was one of seven students who had been admitted to the school at the same time Kaito, Jôi, Xiao Long, and Ayano had.

Soon after he arrived, he'd started picking fights with the group of bullies who had reigned over Kikyo ga Oka Junior High up till that point. What's more, Jun had sent a gorilla named Terada, formerly the big boss of the school bullies, to the hospital, meaning Todoroki now occupied the position of boss monkey.

"Yeah? What's so big about Jun Todoroki?" They probably thought invoking the boss monkey's name would intimidate him, but Kaito didn't bat an eyelash.

Naturally.

Kaito was a psychic.

He was a pyrokineticist, or psychoburner, to be precise, and if he wanted to, he had the power to turn anyone before him into a ball of flame. If his opponents were ordinary human beings, no matter how strong they were, if Kaito went after them with all he had, he would win for sure.

Although you couldn't just go around making a junior high school student into a ball of flame, even if he *was* a punk.

"Hey, you, fine with me! Come on!!"

"Put your head right here and I'll break it for you!" The four others on the ground seemed to get a second wind at the mention of Jun Todoroki's name and surrounded Kaito, shouldering stuff like a golf putter, a police baton, and the kind of extendable metal rod that gets longer when you pull on it.

"Time for you guys to cut it out."

The guy wielding the putter and the one with the police baton turned when their shoulders were tapped.

There stood Jôi, smiling.

"Oh, it's you . . ." Putter Guy, who was trying to say something, got a light push from the palm of Jôi's hand and landed on his butt.

"Ah, ah . . ." He sat there, scared out of his wits, unable to get up.

"Asshole!" Though he was shaking with terror, the guy with the police baton came toward Jôi, swinging it.

But he didn't hit him. That police baton he was so proud of didn't even graze Jôi. All Jôi did was casually move his upper body, one hand still thrust into his pocket. Like a professional boxer, he gracefully dodged the attack, and at the very moment when Police Baton Guy stumbled, Jôi zipped in and whacked him on the temple with his fist. That was all it took for Police Baton Guy's eyes to roll back up in his head and collapse, foaming at the mouth.

If someone who didn't know about Jôi's power had seen this happen, he would probably think Jôi had mastered some special weaponless martial art, and that he'd just used some Chinese Fist of Death thing, the kind that's been transmitted from father to son for four thousand years.

But actually there was an even more amazing explanation.

Jôi was a brilliant psychic who was clairvoyant, prescient, and telepathic. Prescience is seeing what happens in the future, but Jôi's power was even more mysterious. He could see quite clearly the future's next moment—how people in front of him were just about to move before they did it. And he even knew how to attack them so they would "break."

So, of course, some loser with a police baton had no

chance of catching Jôi. Even if he'd had a gun, he'd have no chance.

The fact was that one month ago, during the incident that took place in the middle of the night at this very school, Jôi had, all by himself, fought off ten pursuers with paralyzer guns, in no time at all.

There was no one better to have as an ally, but no one worse to have as an enemy, according to Ayano. That was Jôi Toma, the most powerful genius psychic.

"Want to keep going?" There was no threat in Jôi's expression as he said this, smiling. Contrary to what you might think, this seemed to terrify the hoodlums.

The last three were barely standing. Propping up between them the two who were out cold, they left in confusion, muttering sharp parting remarks.

"Thanks, everybody. I owe you," I said to Kaito and Jôi, and also Ayano, who was still inside my head.

"Aw, c'mon, what're you talking about, freak?" Kaito threw a reckless arm around my shoulders. "If you'd flipped out like that last time, all hell would've broken loose."

Kaito was talking about the psychic battle that had taken place at this school one month before. A powerful psychic sent from the Greenhouse, Takemaru, had unleashed—and lost control of—his powers of psychokinesis, reducing a wooden gymnasium to rubble. But Takemaru and I, who had been in the gym at the time, had been miraculously spared from injury. Kaito and the others thought I had managed this with psychokinesis.

Thinking back on it, my life was totally different now from that time one month ago when Ayano had projected her out-of-body self into my room.

Here's how my life had been up until that point. I'd get up at seven-thirty, brush my teeth, wash my face, then, after consuming, slowly and with relish, a breakfast of toast, vegetable juice, and an egg sunny-side up, I'd fly out of the house at the last minute in a panic.

And then I'd space out during class as the teacher's hand moved over the chalkboard, all the time thinking about something totally different. Mostly I'd imagine that I was a hero, journeying through a world of magic and monsters. After school, I was out of the classroom before the bell stopped ringing and headed straight home. At home, I'd carelessly leave my shoes wherever I took them off, announce to whomever that I was home, then go up to my room on the second floor to make notes on the figurines I'd thought up while at school and start to draw illustrations of them in my sketch book.

After that, I'd use the "Kakeru" figure I'd made, the princess, and the mages, and act out a play I'd made up (based a little bit on fact) using my little study desk as the stage, with me as the only actor and audience.

Now it had been more than a month since I'd played with my figurines.

Not that I was trying to act grown-up. I hadn't graduated from these things and shut up the figures carefully in a drawer, but I could never tell when a genuine adventure might start up again, so I didn't have time for imaginary games.

"We want you to use your power as little as possible, Kakeru, because your power has too much impact," this from Jôi.

Uh, no it doesn't (sweat drops).

Jôi knew everything, from what was right around the corner to what people were thinking, and here he was, under the mistaken impression that my ultra-luckiness was a supernatural power.

But I couldn't bring myself to say it now, and even if

Jôi told me "You're not a psychic or anything, just an ordinary ninth grader," it would sure be a load off my shoulders to say something like, "You're right. I'm sorry. But I didn't lie to you. You guys decided on your own that's what I was."

"I'm late. Sorry. Is the fight over already?" Xiao Long rushed up. Xiao Long disliked fights and had probably taken his time so as not to join in.

Ayano was looking out and beckoning from the window of a second-floor classroom. "Kakeru! Jôi, Kaito, Xiao Long, let's eat our lunches together!"

"All right! You don't have to shout. Geez!" Even thinking I might get dirty looks and maybe more from those jealous punks again, I was feeling pretty good.

"Okay, let's go eat," said Kaito, with a big yawn.

"It was Xiao Long's turn to make the lunches, wasn't it," said Jôi.

"Today we have spicy tofu in brown sauce and pot stickers." Xiao Long's Chinese food lunches were the real deal.

The four of them now lived in a rented house, paid for with money Jôi had used his prescience to win in the lottery. Who made the meals and who did the cleaning changed every day. They lived together a life of freedom and ease impossible for the average junior high school student. And I was invited over every day after school as one of them, for relaxing times away from the prying eyes of adults.

Eating, drinking, goofing around.

Just as if we'd been friends for years.

Kaito, the pyrokineticist who could produce flames; Xiao Long, who used *qigong*; Jôi, who was prescient; and Ayano, who had the gift of out-of-body projection.

I was the one with the power of psychokinesis.

Of course, I had no such power.

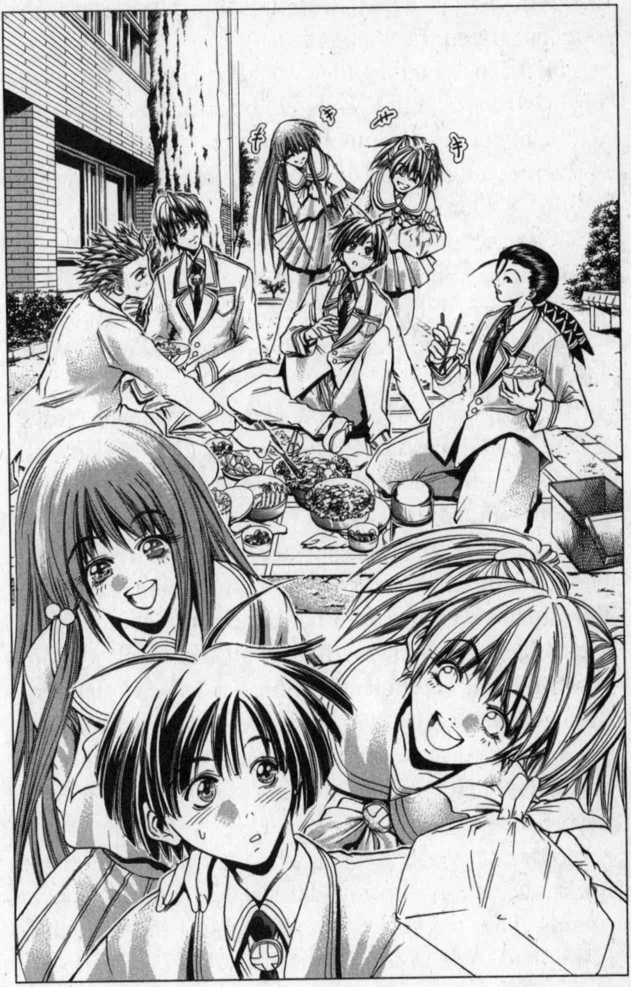
キ
キ
キ

I was just an extremely ordinary fourteen-year-old junior high school student.

It was just that these one-in-a-million miracles kept happening and I kept defeating real psychics, so everyone had gotten the wrong idea.

I felt bad not telling them that I had no psychic powers like they did, but I wanted to be one of them for just a little bit longer. Eventually, when they found out I was just a pretend psychic, they would probably go away.

But just for now . . .

"Geez, it took you so long I came down by myself!" Ayano's face appeared before mine.

"Oh, sorry. I'll just go get my lunch."

"It's right here, Kakeru." But it wasn't Ayano who held out my bag.

It was Sayaka Mamidori. Her name meant "truly green." And she was Beautiful Girl No. 2, the talk of my class—no, of the school—who had transferred into my class the same day Ayano had.

Her eyes were large, her nose was small, her chin perfectly rounded, and even though she didn't do anything to her eyebrows, they had a pleasant right-left symmetry. Her hair didn't seem to be bleached, but instead had a natural chestnut hue. She was tall and slender, but not *too* tall. Her face was so petite that if a normal girl stood next to her, it would mess up your sense of perspective. Her skin was so fair it looked as if it had never seen the sun.

As transfer students who had started at the school on the same day, Ayano and Sayaka had become close friends. The two of them walking down the street together had such an impact that any male ranging from child to adult would turn around to look at them.

"Sayaka wants to eat with us, too. Is that okay?" this from Ayano.

"It's okay, isn't it, Kakeru?" Sayaka cocked her head slightly as she smiled. Did I mention her smile was as beautiful as Ayano's?

"O-of course it is!" I looked at Ayano while I answered.

I was expecting one of those "Stop acting like a lovesick boy!" reactions right out of a romantic comedy, but Ayano didn't seem jealous at all and was looking around for a place to eat lunch.

"Hey, there, are you the girl in Ayano's class everyone's talking about?" asked Kaito.

"What do you mean 'the girl everyone's talking about,' Mister Himuro?!" Sayaka hit Kaito playfully on the shoulder.

"Ow. You sure are cheerful," said Kaito and laughed.

"This is nice. Lunch is going to be good." Xiao Long was enjoying himself.

Jôi laughed, too, but he seemed distracted. Something was bothering him. His lunch unfinished, he said, "There's something I have to take care of," and he abruptly went off.

Akira Hiyama was standing on the school's roof.

Idly she twined her fingers in the chain-link fence, gazing at the misty blue mountain range in the distance. Noticing the faint lipstick mark on the can of protein shake she'd been drinking instead of lunch, she wiped her mouth with the back of her hand.

Since returning to "her place of employment" part-time, she'd started wearing the makeup that she'd shut away in a drawer over a year ago. It was good to wear skirts and put on lipstick again, because it made her less conspicuous when she worked undercover.

Usually, however, when she returned to school to resume her janitorial duties, she carefully washed it all off. But today there hadn't been time. She licked her lips and sensed the lipstick's perfume. It felt uncomfortable. It was at times like this when she felt it would be better to have been born a man.

"Late! Geez!" Irritated, she twisted the can from which she had finished drinking into the wire mesh.

There was someone she was here to talk to, but they hadn't set a time because the other party was not someone for whom that was necessary.

He would have foreseen that she had something she wanted to talk to him about and just come. One who knew the future, who could read the minds of others. A young man who, in a different time, might have been worshipped as a child of God.

Hiyama was waiting for Jôi Toma.

"Sorry to keep you waiting, Hiyama-san." Hiyama was not surprised to hear Jôi say that as he appeared.

Jôi had scored one hundred percent on a test of foresight using cards. He would write down in advance what card Hiyama would pick, seal it in an envelope, and Hiyama would keep it. And when she chose a card and compared it with his prediction on the paper in the envelope, it always matched, no matter how many times she tried it.

"What about Kakeru and the others?" Hiyama asked, turning around.

"They're still eating lunch. I want to get back quickly, so please . . ." Jôi gave a childlike smile.

"What're you going to do when you go back?"

"Nothing. I just want to be with them because it's lunchtime."

"Humph. That's not like you."

"I am a fourteen-year-old junior high school student, too. Isn't that normal?"

"But would a fourteen-year-old junior high school student say that?"

"Hiyama-san . . ." Jôi smiled wryly. "Why do you treat me like this?"

"What do you mean, 'this'?"

"Not like anyone else. Please treat me more like a child. If you don't, I'll turn into a bad boy?" He softened his statement by making it sound like a question.

Jôi had come up beside her and looked into her eyes from the corners of his. Warily putting some distance between them, Hiyama answered, "You yourself know best why I can't treat you like a child."

"I do not know."

"How can that be? Read my mind."

"Hiyama-san. If you think I can always read someone's mind, or see the future, you're mistaken. I am not God. I'm human."

"You scored one hundred percent on the test with cards for reading the future."

"That's not 'the future.' If all you have to do is raise the probability, anyone can do it with practice. Even you, Hiyama-san."

"Then what about when we were attacked by Farmers? You dodged bullets with one hundred percent accuracy and overpowered a bunch of big brawny guys with one blow."

"But that was—"

"How can that same guy pretend he doesn't know about Kakeru?"

"What about Kakeru?"

"Don't play innocent. He's not a psychic. All that incredible stuff that happened last month was just a fluke. A bunch of coincidences just piled up on each other, making it look like he defeated the bad guys with psychokinesis."

"That's not true."

"What?"

"Kakeru *is* a psychic. And an unbelievably strong one—no, that's not the way to say it. More of a special kind . . . in some ways, he's dangerous."

"Dangerous? Him? Hah, that can't be—"

"It's true. To his enemies . . . possibly even to us."

"Stop exaggerating," Hiyama drew close to Jôi. "If there's something you know, then come on out and say it! If you don't, then I'll get to thinking—"

Putting his index finger in front of Hiyama's lips as if to intercept her words, Jôi said, "Would you stop talking about this?"

Hiyama was shocked. She brushed away Jôi's hand before she'd had a chance to think.

"Ow!" The metal of her watch struck Jôi and he winced.

"Oh. I'm sorry. It was an accident." Hurriedly, Hiyama squeezed Jôi's hand. Blood oozed from where he'd been nicked by the watch.

"Why didn't you avoid that? You can dodge bullets . . ."

"I just didn't know. That's all."

"Huh?"

"The reason I can avoid attacks from my enemies is that they level their evil intention at me. Most wild animals have the power to avoid danger in the future. I think it's like that. But I don't really understand it." Frowning sadly as he said this, Jôi did look like a normal fourteen-year-old boy. Just that his expression was a little more adult, and he was as lovely as a sculpture.

"There was no malice in your hand just now. Rather, I felt you give off an emotion that was just the opposite. So I couldn't read it at all."

The opposite of malice?

To unexpectedly be told this by a boy more than twelve years younger than she embarrassed Hiyama. She let go of Jôi's hand and put another step of distance between them. She said brusquely, "You're okay, right? This cut's not so bad."

"Yeah. I'm fine. So, what did you want to talk to me about? You didn't want to meet me alone just to talk about this, did you?"

"Of course not. I want to ask you something. I want to know what your game is. You know a crisis is coming. I want to know why you're just sitting back watching, without telling your friends." Hiyama got straight to the point.

But Jôi's expression didn't change. "Do you mean the students who transferred to this school at the same time we did?"

"Oh, come on, you know! There are always a lot of people moving to this area, but eleven, including you, is too many for this time of year. Excluding you four, I checked the other seven in my own way, and it looks like five of them—"

"I don't know either."

"What?"

"I can't get there. It's like it's behind a locked door. At times like this I choose to wait."

"Wait? For what?"

"For something to happen. Now, if you'll excuse me . . ."

"Sometimes it's too late after something happens, Mr. Can-see-the-future," Hiyama muttered to his retreating back.

Having investigated at her place of employment, Hiyama knew the identities of the five. She also knew all the boys and girls had no relatives, and the fact that they had all disappeared almost a year before transferring to this junior high school.

Something was going to happen. Hiyama was not a psychic, but she felt the premonition keenly. All she could do was watch and wait.

Until the "something" Jôi mentioned took place.

We sat on a corner of the school lawn and took out our lunches.

Saying he had something to do, Jôi gave his mostly uneaten lunch to Kaito before going off somewhere.

"He's always doing this, going off by himself, that guy," said Kaito. "He goes off like a stray cat, without telling us why. Well, whatever. At least today I get his lunch. Two lunches. Yum."

"Geez, Kaito, you eat too much," Ayano rebuked Kaito as he dug in greedily.

"Leave some for Jôi. Because usually when he goes off by himself like this, he's doing something for us."

"She's right, Kaito. If you're still hungry, you can have mine." Xiao Long put some of his own fried rice into Kaito's empty lunch box.

Kaito gulped it down at once. "Christ, you guys think too highly of Jôi. He's not the person you think he is. He's the same as us. It's just that he knows everything, so it can't be helped . . ."

Saying something he shouldn't have earned him an elbow in the ribs from Ayano.

He seemed to have forgotten that Sayaka Mamidori was with them.

Kaito laughed to cover up his slip, "Uh, ha ha ha. That guy is *so* smart. Like with arithmetic. He knows *everything*. It's a good thing, too, helps out an idiot like me. Ha ha ha ha." He forced a smile.

He could have at least said "math."

But that's the kind of guy Kaito was. Because for a

long time he'd been the leader of a group of dropouts in a lawless district in Yokohama known as the Nationless Quarter. He probably hadn't gone to junior high school then, naturally. But neither the others nor I had asked, and none of them dared talk about it.

Now that I thought about it, Jôi was a big mystery, too. He hadn't been going to school for at least a year, yet when he was tested soon after being admitted, he was at the top of the class in math, Japanese, and English. When I asked Jôi if he'd used psychometry or anything, he emphatically denied it, so maybe it truly was his own ability.

What *was* Jôi's past, anyway.

"Um, Kakeru?" Sayaka Mamidori interrupted my thoughts as she whispered in my ear, having, at some point, come to sit next to me.

"This is a rumor, but I heard that Jôi Toma and Kaito Himuro, and that seventh grader . . . Xiao Long? They all live in the same house as Ayano, don't they? Are they related? Or are they . . ."

My classmates asked me this all the time. It was probably because I was with them a lot, but I really didn't know how to answer. All I could say was "I've never asked" or "I don't know" or give them the runaround as I saw fit, but . . .

Of course, relatives! That was a great way to answer.

From now on, I'd say that.

If you said they were relatives, you could somehow explain everything, why their surnames were different, why they didn't look alike, why they were all the same age, how one could be Chinese, and one of them half Japanese. Even if only just barely.

"Oh, of *course* they are! There was some kid who said it might be some weird religion, which was kind of scary. I'm so relieved!"

I laughed. "Of course it's not. How could it be?"

"You are right. But if it had been, you're the one who would get my attention."

"Huh? Why me?"

"Cuz I can understand why they're close—they're transfer students and related, but why are *you* so close with them? You've been going to our junior high school for a long time. But it'd make sense if you were all members of the same religion and had the same beliefs."

"Oh, uh, what do I say here . . . I'm related to them, too! Yeah, they're relatives!" It was a forced answer.

"Oh, uh huh? I see . . ."

"Y-yeah. When I asked in detail, Ayano, I mean Fujimura, is my dad's younger brother's niece. So I'm related to them all, somehow." I laughed again. The story was kind of crazy and forced, but laughing and telling her a good story was the only thing I could do.

"That's good."

"Huh?"

That took me unawares. Sayaka Mamidori moved still closer and whispered in my ear, "I'm glad you're not Ayano's boyfriend."

I was flabbergasted. My eyes grew wide. She flew away from me quickly and went over to Ayano, who hadn't yet finished her lunch.

Wh-what did *that* mean? What she just said . . . She didn't mean . . . ?

No way. Not that.

I mean, I'd hardly said two words to her since she'd transferred from wherever one month ago. Plus, Kaito and Jôi were both better-looking than me. Taller, too.

"Hey, Sayaka. It looked like you were having a pretty intense conversation with Kakeru. What were you talking about?" Ayano asked Sayaka, darting glances at me—who looked as though I'd been slapped—from the corner of her eye.

"A secret."

A s-secret. Saying it like that, didn't that make it even more suggestive?

"*Really?* What secret? C'mon, Kakeru, tell me, what were you talking about?"

"N-nothing. Just making small talk . . ."

"Hmm . . ." Ayano flopped down on the grass and shut her eyes. Her chin softened, as if she had fallen asleep. The next moment, Ayano was "inside" me.

What were you talking about? Tell me the truth!

Startled, I did my level best not to think about those last words Sayaka had whispered in my ear.

I mean, I *said* it was nothing! I answered, facing Ayano inside my head.

If it was nothing, then tell *me!*

Um, okay. We were just talking about rumors going around class about why you and I are always together.

Humph . . . Is that it?

Huh? Why?

Because if that's all it was, then there's no reason to say it's a secret.

Well, that's um, uh . . .

Ayano's voice exploded inside my head.

Tell me honestly!

All right, already!

Finally . . . Well?

Uh . . . well, um . . . Sayaka, uh . . . How should I answer? No, if I thought about that, she'd know.

This was really hard.

Sayaka said what?

Um, well, I mean . . .

How should I put this?

Spit it out!

Okay, okay!

She was thinking that maybe you and I are boyfriend-girlfriend.

She was?

I wasn't lying. She really said that. It was just that the nuance was a little different.

You and me?

Uh huh, yeah. Ha ha ha. I wonder why she thought such a thing.

Ayano was silent.

What's wrong, Ayano? Say something, *please.*

Suddenly, Ayano, who appeared to be sleeping on the grass (she was actually projecting herself out of body) sat bolt upright and looked at me.

Then she pulled up Sayaka Mamidori, who had been talking to Xiao Long, by the hand and ran off with her. Wh-what kind of reaction was that? Did she not want to be my girlfriend that much? No, on the contrary, maybe embarrassed?

Oh, forget it.

If only I could read minds like Jôi could. But the moment I thought that, I had second thoughts. Knowing the future could be painful.

This is what my dad said when I had asked for a mobile phone: "When you have a cell phone, then you can hear someone's voice whenever you want to, and hear the other person's thoughts whenever you want to with e-mail.

"But then how will you be able to savor in your heart wanting to hear someone's voice, or wondering how that person is feeling?"

When my dad put it that way, I gave up on the cell phone lifestyle.

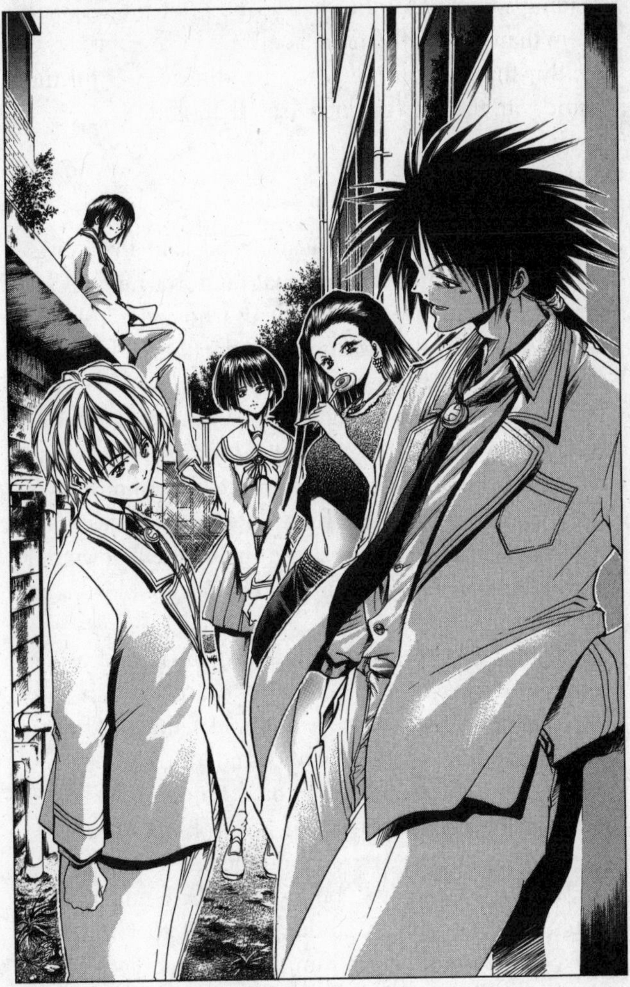

Or rather, I thought maybe I could put off getting one for a while. Of course, it did make it kind of tough to keep company with people who had cell phones. And reading someone's mind had to be a lot more convenient than calling them on a cell.

But there would be really heartbreaking stuff that came with the convenience. Isn't that right?

Jôi . . .

As all the students were heading back to their classrooms, urged on by the bell that rang five minutes before class began, five of the students who had transferred to the school in the last month had gathered behind a school building where there were no people.

The five were Maya Kasuga, Sho Amamiya, Fuyuko Isshiki, Toya Akatsuki, and Jun Todoroki. Each had been honed into a fine psychic at the Greenhouse.

"We should get going. Being late will make us stand out," Maya Kasuga said as she grouchily held down her black, Japanese doll-like hair to keep it from blowing in the wind.

"Nothing to worry about. I'll bring the four of you to someplace under cover close to the classroom one minute before class starts," said Sho Amamiya. The expression on his face was full of confidence.

He was a telepathist who could transport the other four to several different places in the blink of an eye, though it was not as easy as it sounded.

Sho was a Category One psychic who could go into actual combat notwithstanding the fact that this feat had been impossible for him a short time ago. However, in the last month, Sho's ability had increased so much that even he had trouble believing it, as if the trouble he had had progressing before had been a lie.

And it wasn't just Sho. It was the same for Maya. Recently, she, too, had made amazing progress.

Sho's hand closed around the pill case in his pants pocket. As long as they kept using this new drug developed by Ikushima, their abilities would not decline. No, on the contrary, they would only become more powerful.

"I'll walk," said Toya Akatsuki, throwing Sho a scornful look.

"You don't need to hurry so much, either, do you, Maya? No one's going to find out what we're doing, even if we're a little late to class."

"You don't get it, do you, Toya. Jôi's with those guys over there. And also that naturally occurring psychokineticist, Kakeru Hase, who I fought with before."

"Oh, you mean you're scared, don't you?"

"Toya! You've got some mouth on you, considering you're in seventh grade!"

Toya laughed. "Puh-lease!" he said coldly. "You make me laugh. Really. So what if I'm only in the seventh grade? What grade I am in school doesn't have anything to do with the psychic powers I have, does it? In this world, how powerful you are is the only thing that decides your rank. That's why it's easy, isn't it? Right?"

"You little brat . . ." Maya began to concentrate her thoughts.

"You'd better cut it out. You can't beat me. Even if you are at your best now. Want to try?"

"Bring it on!"

"Cut it out," said a slight, sharp-eyed youth sitting on the ground.

Slowly, he rose to his feet, "What's going to happen if we fight among ourselves? Huh?" His voice was quiet, but somehow compelling.

"All right, Jun," Toya said with respect. "I wasn't really going to go for it anyway."

Jun Todoroki turned his face the other way in seeming unconcern. "It's time to break this up. We're done talking. I'm finished communicating things from Ikushima. It's starting . . . finally," and he looked up at the sky.

Just then, it happened.

Jun Todoroki disappeared from sight. Leaving behind a gust of wind.

Sho Amamiya could not believe his own eyes.

"He disappeared? Then that means . . . he must be a . . ."

Until quite recently the name Jun Todoroki had been kept top secret at the Greenhouse, because he was the sole naturally occurring psychokineticist the Farmers had found.

Unlike Takemaru Hidama, who had developed his power of psychokinesis using drugs and electroshock therapy machines, Jun Todoroki had been a powerful psychokineticist from the start. They'd heard from Ikushima that many of the Farmers who had found him died trying to bring him to the Greenhouse.

"I thought he was a PK user. Why does Jun Todoroki have the same power I do?"

"What he just used wasn't teleportation, Sho." Fuyuko snickered again.

"What?"

"That was psychokinesis. He just whooshed away really fast, that's all."

"How could that be? He disappeared, I'm sure of it," exclaimed Maya.

"It just *looked* like he disappeared, Maya. His power is enormous. He merely accelerated to top speed all at once and flew up in the sky, faster than the eye can follow."

Sho and Maya wordlessly exchanged glances.

"Well, shall we go, Fuyuko? We have to hurry or we'll be late for class."

Fuyuko didn't answer.

She just stood still, her pale, expressionless face like that of a doll's, muttering some words like a spell.

"Oh shoot, there she goes again, off in her own little world. Well, whatever, I'm going on without her."

Toya quickly headed toward his class without Fuyuko.

Fuyuko noticed, snapped out of it, and bobbed her head at Sho and Maya before hurrying off after him.

"What do you think about that guy's power? Can he really do that with psychokinesis?"

"If he can, then the guy's too risky. He's a monster — and that's no joke."

In addition to being dangerous, why had a monster who had been shut up in a concrete pen been sent here?

No, more than anything, why did someone like him, who must want freedom, do as the Farmers ordered and remain here in this junior high school like they said?

Sho and Maya, who hadn't been given any explanation but were merely following instructions, began to feel they were on shaky ground.

Something terrible was about to begin.

Something Sho and Maya didn't know about, although they were supposed to be part of this group.

"Man, if only Takemaru was here, he used PK, too. Right, with these new pills, he'd be better than any Jun Todoroki."

"Oh, stop it. Takemaru's a traitor. Didn't Ikushima tell us that he turned on us — his comrades — and joined the enemy?"

"I know. But, like . . ."

"Let's get going, too. Ikushima told us not to stand out."

"There's not much more noticeable than having five of us transfer into the same school all at once, at least *I* don't think so."

"That's for sure."

"What's Mr. Ikushima's plan? Something he can't even tell *us*?"

Maya didn't answer. She felt an unease that she hadn't felt since her psychic battle with the wild type one month before, an unease she couldn't express. Even so, there was nothing she could do but act on what the Farmers—what Arata Ikushima—said to do.

Otherwise it could be that she'd lose this mighty "power" she'd finally obtained. If that happened, they'd have no place to go. None of them had any relatives. If they lost everything that this power had given to them, how would they live? Sometimes this thought plagued them like a panic attack. What spurred them on to fight was not right and wrong. It was fear.

Ikushima, who had cultivated Maya's and Sho's powers, told them that the Greenhouse was made to create a society in which people with psychic powers would be at the center.

But deep down, Maya didn't completely believe this to be true. She could only be certain that Ikushima and the others were trying to change something in this worst of worlds. Right now, she just had to have faith and carry through with this arduous task Ikushima had given them.

Or so Maya kept telling herself.

CHAPTER 3

A NEW TRAGEDY

The event that drove me toward the abyss of despair started that day after school.

Usually I stopped by Ayano's after school, but that day it was my turn for library duty, so I said good-bye to everyone right after class and headed for the school library.

Thinking back on it, it was the worst day of my life.

Before going to the library, I decided to call home to let them know when I'd get back. Since I didn't have a cell, I always stopped by Hiyama-san's janitor's room and used her phone.

When I arrived, Hiyama-san was in the middle of her exercise regimen. "Get your mom to buy you a cell phone," she said, and gave me a flick on the forehead with her thumb and middle finger.

"It's not like that. Not owning a cell phone is part of my personal philosophy," I said. Rubbing where she'd thwacked me, I pushed the buttons for my home phone number on her old-fashioned touchtone phone.

"Hase residence," my older sister answered.

"Oh, Suzue? This is Kakeru. I'm going to be late today because I have library duty. I'm barely going to make it in time for dinner, but I will be there, so would you tell Mom?"

After I'd stated my business in one burst of breath, she said, "Hey, Kakeru, have you done something bad?" in a voice that was unusually dark.

"Huh? Something bad?"

"Something the police might want to talk to you about."

"What do you mean? I wouldn't do something like that, would I?" I returned, in a voice higher than usual, taken aback at the vague and sudden question.

"Of course not. But . . ."

"But what?"

"Oh, nothing, forget it. I'll tell you about it when you get home, so get here as soon as you can, okay?"

"All right. Bye," I said as I put the phone down.

I hadn't been up to anything I shouldn't be yesterday, the day before, or before that. Much less something that the police might want to talk to me about, but, wait a minute! Could they mean Ayano and the others? No, not that Ayano and the others had done something bad. I was thinking instead of their pursuers.

"What, Kakeru, is something wrong?" Hiyama-san looked questioningly into my face. Nervously, I laughed instead of answering right away.

"No, it's nothing. Thanks for letting me use the phone, Hiyama-san. See you. I've got to go do library duty." I gave her an awkward salute before running out of the janitor's room, and headed for the library. It was only four o'clock, but the library was already empty.

It was as still as death.

Well, if they were this short of "customers," then they didn't need someone in the library, now did they?

A sigh escaped me. "*Boring.* And there's still thirty minutes until closing time," I muttered to myself. "If I'm going to spend time here after school, maybe I should read a book."

Right. Were there any books on psychics? For a while now I'd been wondering about psychic powers, what scientists thought about them, if any government organizations were researching them, so this was a perfect chance for me.

"Hey, there's one!" I found a book called *Psychic* on the bookshelves among the books and magazines. It was a translation in hardback by someone named Colin Wilson. "Whoa, there're books like this in school libraries?" I picked it up and headed back to my seat.

There were a number of large tables in the library room with chairs lined up around them, dining table–style. Students sat staggered across from each other at these big tables, poring over the books they'd chosen for fun or research. Nearly every school library was set up like this. Public libraries were the same.

I wondered why. Was it a bad thing to have individual, isolated tables and chairs like you had in a classroom? I thought as I opened the dark green cover.

"*Psychic?*" a voice came from behind me unexpectedly.

Startled, I turned around. Sayaka Mamidori had come up behind me unawares and was peering over my shoulder into the book.

"Sa-Sayaka! What brings you here? I can help you if you're looking for a book. I've got library duty today . . ."

"Uh uh, I'm not looking for anything, I just came here today . . . wow, interesting book. 'Psychics' are people with psychic powers, right?"

She brought her face in close and peered in. Her hair was kind of long. It tickled my cheek.

I felt a shock. Suddenly Sayaka's earlier words came back to me. "So you're not Ayano's boyfriend. I'm glad."

I must have heard her wrong.

I mean, it was *impossible*. I'd hardly even spoken to her. I was only just beginning to think clearly as time passed. But now she was standing so close . . .

Oh, come on. *Kakeru, you're such an idiot! I have Ayano, don't I?*

I couldn't believe I could be so fickle, but in any case, Sayaka was totally out of my league.

"Hey, you want to walk home together?" Sayaka said, tugging on me by the arms.

"Huh? I can't, I've got library duty today, and it's not over ye . . ."

She studied my flustered face with amusement. "It's okay, don't worry about it. No one's here, and no one's going to be angry with you if you go home. Not to mention there've been a lot of scary goings-on recently. There isn't a lot of pedestrian traffic around here, so I want you to walk me home."

"Uh, okay. It's okay with me."

She was so *cute*. She had the kind of face I liked, friendlier and more accessible than Ayano's, which, because of her German blood, seemed a little too . . . orderly. Oh, no, what was I saying?

Lately I'd really been pushing it! If I thought Ayano and this girl had a crush on someone like me, that could only be a big mistake.

Don't think like that! If something sounds too good to be true, then it is!

I was just an ordinary guy with extraordinary good luck. This was what was going through my head when I sluggishly pulled Sayaka up from her chair. "C'mon, let's go home!" I said, and started walking.

On that day, of all days, there was no one in the path to the front gate of the school. I didn't see a single student goofing off on the school grounds.

"Look, you brought home a book that you didn't sign for on your library card!" I said to Sayaka as I led her by the hand.

"Never mind about that," said Sayaka. "You're the guy on library duty. I'll just go and sign it out tomorrow. But to change the subject, can we stop off someplace on the way home? Even the McDonald's in front of the station, or a convenience store, would be okay."

Umm. What'll I do?

Out of consideration I had called home to say I was going to be late, so I figured I'd better find someplace to kill some time.

"Let's stop off someplace, 'kay? And then we can read that book together," Sayaka pointed at the thick book with the dark green cover under my arm.

"This book? It's a book about psychic powers like ESP. Do you have an interest in this subject, Sayaka?"

"Mmm, kind of. Do you know a lot about it?"

"No, not much."

While we were talking about that, we came to the school's front gate. Then, "Hey, Kakeru."

I looked in the direction of the voice calling my name.

For a second I didn't know who it was even after I saw his face.

This was because I'd only ever seen him in jeans and a T-shirt or something similar, even in winter, so it was my first time seeing him in a proper suit with his hair neatly combed.

It was Mamoru Kamichika, my older sister's boyfriend.

He was too cool a boyfriend for my sister to have. I'd only met him two or three times. One time he'd come to visit, and one time I'd run into them in town when they were on a date, and that was about it. Either he was really busy, or he was just playing around with Suzue.

"Mr. Kamichika, what're you doing here? My sister's at home."

I thought Suzue's boyfriend visiting me at school was pretty ridiculous, but Mr. Kamichika didn't seem to be worried about that. "Actually I didn't come here today as Suzue's . . . uh, I mean Suzue's, y'know, 'acquaintance.' "

"Huh?"

Just when I figured I'd better not hold back, two other guys approached me. And it looked like all three guys had business with me. Kamichika was the only good-looking one. The other two, not to put too fine a point on it, looked like thugs.

"Actually, I came here today as a police detective from the Juvenile Division. I'd like to ask you some questions."

"P-police detective? No way, Mr. Kamichika, you want to ask *me* questions?"

It was only then that I recalled what my sister had just asked me. She'd asked me if I'd done anything the police would need to talk to me about. Now I knew why.

Mindful of the two who had been intently watching us the whole time, Kamichika said, "Think you could come down to the station? We'd like to ask you about a certain incident that took place last night."

"An incident . . . from last night . . . ?"

Could it be that Jôi, or one of his enemies, had done something?

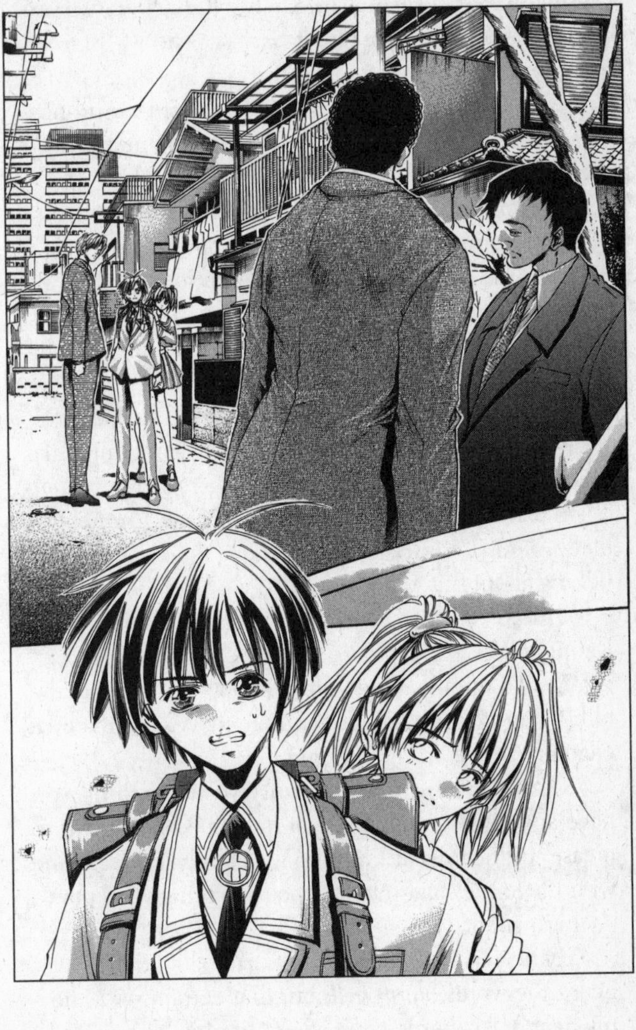

"Wh-what happened, did someone get burned up, or someone jump?" I blurted out.

Kaito's pyrokinesis, or Xiao Long's *qigong*? Mr. Kamichika's face went pale, and the other two exchanged glances. I looked at Sayaka, who was staring, openmouthed.

We'd just been talking about occult stuff. And now Mr. Kamichika was here with these weird questions. I'd have a lot of explaining to do that night.

Sayaka was the least of my worries at the moment.

The younger of the two thugs pushed past Mr. Kamichika. "Could you tell us more about that?" he said, drawing closer.

"W-wait a minute, he's a boy, fourteen years old. You can't treat him like a hardened criminal," said Mr. Kamichika. Maybe he was as nice a guy as he looked.

But this is not the time to be saying something like that, is it? Meanwhile, Thug Jr. was the exact opposite.

"This is more than a juvenile crime. Somebody died! *And* in an interrogation room at the station, while talking about this kid!"

"Huh? W-what are you talking about? Mr. Kamichika?"

"Wait a minute. Pardon me, I know this kid. Let me talk to him." His shoulders hunched, Mr. Kamichika edged in between Thug Jr. and me.

"Okay, Kakeru. Calm down. We don't think you have anything to do with what happened last night, so please just hear what I have to say calmly. Please come with me to the station to tell me everything you know."

I was silent.

My heart was racing like an alarm bell. I'd only ever heard the words *alarm bell*, but that certainly was how my heart felt—*hurry, panic, flee!*—it urged me.

"Now, I can hardly believe this myself" was how Mr.

Kamichika began his story, and then he summarized the tragic events of the night before.

"Lately, kids in this neighborhood, about your age, have been disappearing one after another. Well, only kids who have problems at home, so at first we thought it was just a coincidence that there were so many runaways at once. But last night we found one of them.

"We discovered her under bizarre circumstances. She was surrounded by a gang of punks. They were on the ground, and they looked as if they'd been savaged by a gorilla . . ."

Attacked by a gorilla?

Psychokinesis?

"Well, naturally, we thought someone had tried to save this girl but had gone too far, and run away from the scene. But now we don't think that's what happened."

"Why?" I asked, even though I knew the answer. The girl had done it, I was sure of it. She was a psychic.

"Well, let me tell you the rest at the station," Mr. Kamichika darted his eyes at his thuggish partners, who were beginning to look exasperated.

"No," I said.

My chest was still ringing like an alarm bell. But until I heard more about what happened, I had absolutely no intention of moving one inch.

Not too long ago I would have thought the story was crazy. But now it was all too easy to imagine what kind of "power" had done it . . . now that I'd been exposed to Takemaru's terrible psychic power. So I wanted to ask. Here and now.

"Please tell me more about what happened while we're here. If you don't, I won't go to the station with you."

"R-right, Kakeru. This is the craziest thing I've ever

heard, a false accusation. You must not go. And you don't even know if they're really police detectives." Sayaka's assumption was a little off and she was angry. But at the sound of her voice, my heart grew stronger.

Oh! Sorry, Ayano . . . oh, geez, at a time like this, what was I thinking?!

"That's what we've got. Is it okay if we talk to him here?" Mr. Kamichika asked the older thug with a sigh.

Geezer Thug said nothing, only nodded.

Again Mr. Kamichika began to speak. "The girl was taken into protective custody by a beat cop. After that she was in a station interrogation room for two hours. She wouldn't speak no matter what I asked, then all of a sudden . . ." Mr. Kamichika's story was shocking.

She'd said she was the one who half-killed the punks, then burst out babbling incoherently, as if she was possessed by evil spirits.

You don't have to believe me. I have obtained amazing power! Amazing power . . .

The girl's eyes rolled back in her head and she began to shake. Mr. Kamichika went to the shivering girl and grabbed her by the shoulders. Suddenly an unknown force had blown all six feet of him back two and a half yards. Then for real, her face had blown up like a balloon. The last thing she said clearly was the name "Kakeru Hase," and then her head exploded like a dropped watermelon.

I was speechless.

No way was I involved in a horror story like this. I knew better than anyone.

But.

Why had my name come up?

Mr. Kamichika gave another deep sigh. "You may not believe this, but all this happened right in front of me. It's not something I should tell a civilian, especially someone underage like you. But it's just too weird . . . if you include what happened after . . ."

"Something happened after?"

"Yeah. The girl's body disappeared. In just the time it took me to leave the interrogation room to get some help, it had disappeared, not one drop of blood left."

I was quiet. This was even stranger. It was, of course, all the work of a psychic. But did she do this to herself, or was there someone close by who could use psychokinesis? At that instant I thought of Takemaru. It wouldn't be impossible for him. A guy who can smash a gym to smithereens could have done it.

No, there was a big difference between an old building and a person.

I think Kaito had mentioned it before. Burning stuff was easy, but with his pyrokinetic ability, burning people was impossible. The only person he could burn was himself. So when you heard about people burning up, they were probably people who were pyrokinetic and burned themselves without realizing what they were doing.

By the same logic, she could have made her own head explode.

"You're done, right, Officer Kamichika?" said Thug Jr. as he grabbed my arm where I stood rooted to the spot, stunned.

"Okay, let's go. I told you everything, just like I promised. Even the stuff I'm not supposed to tell people. Come to the station, I have some questions for you."

No. I don't want to go. I know that's what I thought at the time. *Take your hands off me! Go away!*

It was at that very moment that . . .

"Gewa!" An inhuman moan. At the same time, Thug Jr. was thrown back five feet. Then he hit his head on a telephone pole and collapsed.

"Huh?" Even at that distance, I could see that his head was smashed in halfway. Within seconds, the whole area was submerged in blood.

My heart skipped a beat. Was he dead? Did he die right there in front of me? Why?

Not understanding what had happened, the older detective dithered, unable to do anything. A little calmer, Mr. Kamichika got a grasp on the situation and turned toward me.

"D-did you do that?"

I shook my head "no." Shook it emphatically.

No! I would *never* do something like . . .

I wasn't a psychic.

I . . .

"Kakeru! Let's get out of here!" someone yelled. And then they took my hand and started to run.

Oh. Sayaka Mamidori. I'd forgotten she was there. Without knowing why, I started to run. With Sayaka. I had no sense of anyone following.

Don't come after me. Honestly, that's what I prayed. *What if it had been me who killed that young detective just now? Then you, my sister's boyfriend, might be next, Mr. Kamichika.* I ran on, thinking the unthinkable. Sayaka Mamidori and I ran. Like children who had been caught making mischief.

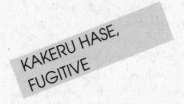

CHAPTER 4

KAKERU HASE,
FUGITIVE

In the last month, Akira Hiyama had quit smoking. Cigarettes robbed you of your stamina and suffocated your brain. As long as she was no more than a school janitor, she hadn't needed to worry, but from now on that wouldn't work.

Every day she retrained her flabby muscles and reflexes for more than an hour. Even now she was doing tough weight training in her janitor's room—with forty-pound free weights. When she'd joined the secret agency, she'd fulfilled the requirements of its tough training program—one that did not have different standards for men and women. At first, every muscle in her body ached, and in the mornings, she could hardly get out of bed. But soon enough, she'd gotten used to hard training again. She no longer even felt out of breath. Though it would take a little longer to get back to her personal best—her days of active service—she was still able to complete almost the entire exercise program.

The unexpected arrival of the young psychics had turned Hiyama's life around. She'd taken on a job that didn't suit her, without caring where it led, only to end up going nowhere. Was it just fate? Or had her script been written ahead of time by persons unknown?

Now that she thought about it, it was her former supervisor who had referred her to this live-in job at Kikyo ga Oka Junior High School, after she'd been forced to leave her previous employers: the Crisis Management Commandos, an unofficial arm of the National Police Agency. Crimers for short. An organization whose existence was officially kept undercover.

Five years ago, her talent had made her so conspicuous at the police academy that she'd left it midterm—even though she had once hoped to become a police officer—to join the Crimers. In her three years at the agency, Hiyama had become the Crimers' top ace. Then why had she retired and become a janitor?

It all began with a case from three years ago. Three detectives from the National Police Agency had gone missing while investigating a mysterious string of disappearances: a number of boys and girls, aged twelve to sixteen, had vanished, one after the other. An internal leak was suspected. Hiyama, representing the Crimers, was dispatched to find the detectives.

But then one of her colleagues at the Crimers disappeared. It was thought he'd been abducted. And that wasn't all: as the case was examined more closely, the clues all pointed to Hiyama as the leak.

In the end, there was no proof that Hiyama was a double agent, so she wasn't fired, merely forced out. And there were limits on where she could work. She wasn't allowed to seek a job in the private sector. That's when Kyosuke Sasaki, her former commanding officer at Crimers, helped her get the janitor's job.

She'd doubted that a former secret agent would make a suitable handyman and nightwatchman at a junior high school. But, deep in despair, she'd simply accepted the job without thinking.

"Whew."

She threw down the weights and flopped down on her back.

"Don't tell me Mr. Sasaki's up to something there in the background . . ." Unintentionally, her suspicions slipped out.

No, it couldn't be, she denied quickly. It was just chance that the psychics had found her, right?

Chance, huh? No one could have known about it beforehand, except God or the Devil, or . . .

Jôi?

"That's not possible . . ." she said to herself. She took off her sweaty T-shirt and tossed it aside.

If she didn't look after these poor kids, something catastrophic would happen. The psychics had two choices: stay in the shadows, or let the world know them for who they really were. If someone else had different plans for those kids, she'd be there to protect them at all costs.

So that was why she, who had dropped out after having been shamed and humiliated, had returned to Crimers once again, even if it was only on a part-time basis.

"Hiyama-san!" A voice came through the door. At the same time, there was a violent knock.

"Who's there?"

"It's Jôi!"

"Um, I'm right in the middle of something. Come back la—" Quickly she looked for a change of clothes.

"I'm coming in!"

"Eek! Hey, wait . . . !" She let out a feminine squeal that did not quite suit her. The door opened while she was still naked to the waist.

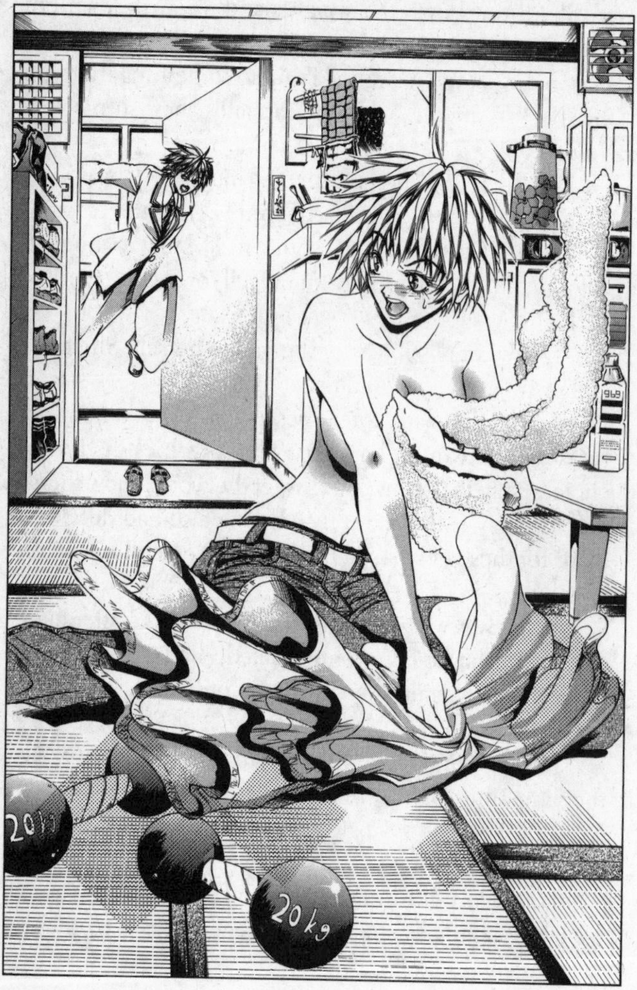
20kg

"Ah! Sorry . . ." Jôi turned away, embarrassed.

"You *idiot*! Did you *forget* that I'm a woman? What kind of idiot just comes barging into someone's room like that?"

"I'm sorry, I was in a hurry."

"What are you saying? I thought you were psychic! Sheesh . . ." She pulled on a T-shirt and then gave Jôi a hard poke to the back of the head.

"And why are you in such a hurry?"

"It's something I . . . saw." Jôi's face looked unusually uneasy.

"Something you saw? What?"

"A beginning. The guy from that last time was doing it. It came into my head clearly. Like a locked door opening . . ."

"What?"

"Kakeru . . ."

"What?"

Hiyama started changing clothes without regard to where she was before Jôi had finished speaking. She faced Jôi, who didn't know where to look, and roared, "Well, what are you waiting for?! Get the others! We've got to look for Kakeru!"

I was in a shack that looked like it might collapse at any moment. I cowered, holding my knees.

It was the same wooden cabin with the galvanized metal roof that Ayano had brought me to one month before, where I first met Xiao Long and the unconscious Jôi. Next to me was Sayaka Mamidori, who had run away with me. I didn't know why I'd come here. It was just that there was no other place to go.

I couldn't go home, of course. I had thought of going to Ayano's place, but that also felt kind of dangerous. Not only would I get them mixed up in all this, I'd probably manage to run into a police officer at the same time.

Man, did I feel like a criminal. Maybe I *was* a criminal. Even if it wasn't a crime to use psychic powers, even if *I* was the one who had killed that detective, then that made me a murderer.

I gave a huge sigh, my head in my hands.

That couldn't be. It had to be a mistake, or a trap someone had devised, I thought after I'd calmed down a little. I was absolutely not a psychokineticist. I mean, I'd tried doing stuff like "Door open!" and "Roll, rock! Come to me!" but nothing happened. No real surprise there.

But then how could I slam someone into a telephone pole five feet away, crushing his head and killing him, without moving so much as my hand?

Oh, what a mental image. *Blurrgh.* I felt sick.

"Kakeru, what are we going to do now?" Sayaka asked. But she didn't seem to be particularly frightened. She was as cheerful as always.

Right before her very eyes, a man had been killed by some unseen power. If I were her, I wouldn't need a better excuse to run home crying, jump into bed, pull the covers over my head, and never come out again.

"What do you mean, what? If we go to my house the police will probably be there." I swallowed the nausea welling up inside.

"We can't stay here forever, now, can we?"

"True, but . . ."

"Right, but what about staying here for a while? That way I can bring you some food. Okay? Let's do that. Stay here."

I looked around and saw straw mats all around. There were stacks of old newspapers, too, and in places the floor was so rotten that it looked like you could fall right through, but if I used the newspapers for a blanket and the straw mats as a bed, I would probably be able to sleep.

I let out another sigh. I'd been sympathetic one month ago when Ayano, Xiao Long, and Jôi had been fugitives, but to think that now *I* was in the same position. Oh, right! What about Ayano and the others? What were they doing now? Did they know what kind of mess I was in?

Of course. Jôi was there, no way would he not notice. They might come save me.

No, they would come for sure. I mean, I was one of them. If I had psychic powers, then now I really was . . . uh, but if I did, then that meant I was a murderer.

I was going around in circles. Noticing that I had fallen silent, Sayaka said, "It's all right, Kakeru. I'm on your side."

"But why?" I surprised myself by putting my doubts into words. "*Why* are you on my side? You and I are just classmates. We met up in the library by chance and decided to go home together and—".

"Is it bad that I'm your ally?"

"It's not bad . . . what I mean is, I'm happy. I just wonder about why."

"You've been on my mind for a while, Kakeru."

Her saying that reminded me of what she'd whispered in my ear earlier. That thing about being happy Ayano wasn't my girlfriend. How could there be any way she could possibly have a crush on me? It was too unreal. There was no way that a girl I'd hardly ever spoken to, especially one who was so pretty and popular, could be in love with *me*.

"But didn't you find it kind of exciting?"

"Huh?"

"We saw a detective get blown away right before our very eyes. It was amazing!"

"What do you mean, 'amazing'?"

That's not how I would have put it.

"Every day is so boring. I just knew that, if I was with you, life would be so much more exciting! Oh, but am I bothering you?"

"No, it's fine. And it's better than being by myself. I think what happened to that detective just now could have been my fault. I might have done that."

"If you did it, that's amazing!"

"Huh?"

"Why, Kakeru, that means you have psychic powers! Just like in that book." Sayaka pointed at the book under my arm, looking all excited. I'd forgotten I still had that little book with the dark green cover.

"It'd be really amazing if it's true! You'd be a superman, Kakeru!"

"But if I really did that thing back there with my powers, then I've committed murder, haven't I?"

"You didn't intend to kill him, did you?"

"No, I didn't."

"Well, then, isn't it more like an accident? Like if you threw the guy who was coming to get you and it just so happened that a truck was coming by and hit him?"

"But isn't that murder?"

"I don't think so. You weren't doing anything. It's the fault of the policeman who tried to arrest you."

"We don't know if I've done anything or not."

"But you didn't know anything about that girl who died at the police station!"

"Of course not. But it looks like she knew *me*." After all, she had called out my name as she died.

"Well, then, you had nothing to do with it, Kakeru.

Haven't you seen those TV shows where people who have split personalities do bad stuff without even knowing it? But it couldn't be that."

"Split personalities?"

I hadn't thought of that. Was it possible? Ayano and the others, including Jôi, thought I had psychic powers. And if it was true, then I had powers I didn't even know about. If so, would it really be that strange if there was *another* me, inside, who had the capacity to do something really evil?

Maybe there was something to the split-personality theory. There had certainly been times when I didn't know what I'd been doing. Of course, it was possible that I'd just forgotten. And there probably weren't many people who could tell you what they'd done three days ago, or one week ago. But wasn't that actually kind of scary?

Suddenly I felt like I didn't know who I was anymore. I stood up, as if to cast that thought aside. But it was no good. I'd decided.

"I'm going to the police."

"What? Why?"

"I'm going to the police and tell them everything I know. If they're going to arrest me, so be it."

"I don't think they *can* arrest you. I mean, you didn't lay a hand on him. I saw the whole thing. I'll be a witness for you."

"Well, that's true, but . . ."

There was logic in what Sayaka was saying. The police couldn't arrest me with the laws like they were now, and of course, even if it went to court, I wouldn't go to jail for the crime of murder.

"Okay? So how about having a little more confidence? Because you really are amazing. If you really do have psychic powers, then you are superior to ordinary people."

I was silent.

"And that's why I am your friend. You are an amazing person. Ooh, my heart's pounding."

Sayaka's smile was inappropriate. I almost sighed. Was that really so? Were psychics superior to ordinary people? It seemed to me that all the psychics I knew had miserable lives. They were all so sad, desperately wanting to live normal lives, but completely unable to.

Take Takemaru for example. Takemaru and I had fought, but by fight I mean I didn't do a thing. Sure, he'd gotten out of control because he'd been ingesting so many strange drugs, but it was really his traumatic childhood, and the emotional damage it did, that drove him to violence.

All the other psychics I knew had had troubled and unusual childhoods, too. And if it was only because they had special powers, then being a psychic was a curse.

Somehow it just didn't seem like psychics were a chosen people, or an evolved race. Think about rabbits. They're really weak. That's why they have those long ears to hear sounds really well even from far away. Maybe it's like that.

"Anyway, for now, I'm going home. If the police are there asking questions, my mom and sisters must be worried. Sayaka, you should go home, too." And then it happened.

"Kakeru, are you in there? Please come out," called a voice with a bullhorn.

Jôi and the others had gathered at Kikyo ga Oka Junior High. It was after school, so they were alone, except for Akira Hiyama.

It was already almost six o'clock, but it was still light out. It was June, and the sun set late. However, they had a feeling they'd be out late. So Hiyama gave each of them flashlights, protein bars, and waist pouches to carry it all.

"And that's how it is, all right, everyone?" Hiyama doled the equipment out and began to leave, fastening her own waist pouch around her middle.

"According to Jôi, Kakeru fled to the hills. We're going to divide and conquer. The sooner we find him the better. If we don't, what'll happen, Jôi?"

"I don't know specifically yet. But it's certain that there will be no going back."

"There will be no going back?" Akira asked.

"Yes. Kakeru may become our enemy."

"*Kakeru?*"

"I'm sure of it. It came to me so powerfully . . . from behind the 'open door.' " Jôi often spoke in metaphors when he talked about what his psychic abilities felt like.

Hiyama, however, was still unable to understand what his words meant. Kakeru was no psychic. Hiyama refused to believe it, no matter what anyone said to her. What did it mean, that the Kakeru she knew might become their enemy? What could Kakeru possibly do? But still, she couldn't disregard Jôi's prediction.

"I called Kakeru's house a little while ago. His mom answered. He's not home yet," Ayano said worriedly.

"It definitely looks like something happened," said Xiao Long.

"Something's happened to our friend. Don't we have to do something? Those guys at the Greenhouse are probably behind it, too, natch." Kaito's rage was already burning hot. It shimmered around him in a haze of heat.

"There is no mistake. Which means we have to do something. It's up to us," Jôi said, and trotted out of the school gates.

The other four followed him. They left the school just as dusk fell.

They were on their way.

The four psychics would take this route. They would seek out Kakeru Hase.

Arata Ikushima was convinced.

Jôi Toma, the psychic prodigy, was with them. With his abilities, he would already have sensed that something was amiss. And that Akira Hiyama woman, who was shielding them, was a Crimer.

"Got it? By no means, don't let any of the five go. Be especially careful of Jôi," commanded Ikushima.

"Shut up, Ikushima. Nothing you can do will help," said Jun Todoroki. He thrust his hands into his pockets as he levitated. As if competing with him, Sho Amamiya repeatedly teleported just enough so that he could soar a little higher.

"I can see them." Toya Akatsuki had his eyes closed. "They are within thirty yards of the forest. Jôi is walking up front. After him are Kaito, Ayano, and Xiao Long. Akira Hiyama is with them, too. Whoa, she has one of those paralyzer guns that the Farmers use. I wonder if she thinks it will work on us. Heh heh heh."

"Sleep in the abyss . . . now is this time . . . for me . . . to use . . . and then . . ." Fuyuko Isshiki muttered something that appeared to be a curse, eyes unfocused.

How is it up there, Sho? Maya's images and voice arrived in Sho's head via telepathy. *Things are perfect here. But I feel kind of uncomfortable, doing what I'm told, but not knowing how things are going to turn out.*

"It's too late to be saying that now. The battle is

going to begin. Our role is to stop them!" Sho said. Then he vanished like an illusion.

"Kakeru! Can you hear me? We know you're inside this cabin! Will you please come out? This is Kamichika!"

I sprang to my feet at the sound of the voice outside the dilapidated cabin. Mr. Kamichika was here. Outside. I peered out through the many holes in the glass. I could see several of what looked like white police officer's helmets about forty feet away in the grass. Mr. Kamichika stood at the head of the group, holding a megaphone.

"The police are here?! Oh, no, they want to arrest you, Kakeru, I know it!" Sayaka hid herself behind my back.

"Perfect timing. I'm going out there. I was going to go to the police anyway." I put a hand on my chest to calm myself.

I had to stay calm, no matter what. If I really had psychic powers, something like what had happened earlier might happen again.

"No, Kakeru! You can't go out there! It's too dangerous!" Sayaka cried.

"It's not dangerous. That detective out there, Mr. Kamichika, is my sister's boyfriend. If I explain everything to him, I think he'll understand."

"But take a good look! Those police officers around him have pistols!"

"Huh?"

It couldn't be, I figured as I looked out of a hole in the window glass.

Sayaka was right. There were more than ten policemen out there, and looking carefully I could see they all had their pistols raised. And they weren't just the usual uniformed police. They were riot police, decked out with metal shields.

"Th-they've gotta be kidding! What did I do?"

Then I realized and stopped mid-sentence. The image of the detective blown back by an unseen force, head crushed, came into my head. Despite everything, I couldn't believe that that had happened because of some power of mine. But if the other detective who was there thought that it had been me, then he probably considered me to be a monster with a weapon more dangerous than any gun.

Of course they weren't going to come for me unarmed. Of course they'd have guns.

I felt the blood leave my face. What would happen if I got shot? Would they shoot me in the head . . . or in the heart? First, there'd be a *bang*, then a hole would open up in my body, then blood would spurt out. Then, after that, burning pain, and then . . . and then . . .

I knew I shouldn't be thinking, but worst-case scenarios kept racing around inside my head.

Bam! Someone kicked the door in.

"Arrgh!" I turned around. A riot policeman holding a gun jumped in right in front of me.

"Kya—h!" screamed Sayaka from behind me.

"Freeze!" roared the policeman. Several more riot police burst in at the same time. All of them had guns trained on Sayaka and me.

And then, all at once my head came to a boil.

I didn't know what was going on. An emotion, like surprise, like fear, like anger ran through my body in a tenth of a second. No. I did not want to die. Who did these guys think they were?

Get out! Disappear!

"Oof!" A groan like someone who had been hit in the stomach. It came from the riot police.

Bakya! Gashyan!

The sound of wood splintering mixed with the sound of glass shattering. Four or five of the muscular riot police in front of me were blown through the wall or glass in front of me and thrown outside. The men flew through space in slow motion.

Terrified and frightened faces. Surprised and confused faces. Already their faces were unconscious, eyes rolled back in their heads.

I stood rooted to the spot, stunned.

This definitely settled it.

I was a psychic. In addition to that, I was a monster possessing psychokinesis strong enough to be able to throw a man and kill him.

Scenes from one month ago flashed before me. My battle with Maya. The car that had come flying when I was in a jam. How I was saved by a sudden gust of wind when I'd fought Sho. All the bullets had missed us when the Farmers were shooting paralyzer guns at us.

And also Takemaru. When his psychokinetic power had run berserk and he destroyed the old wooden gym and we were about to be crushed by the rubble, we'd narrowly escaped death by a one-in-a-million miracle. The rubble had made a dome as if to protect us.

Of course, even back then I'd thought it was strange that miracles like this kept happening, when there was no such thing as miracles.

Or course there hadn't been. All of these deeds had been achieved by my psychokinesis!

"We're going in!" I heard someone's instructions outside the cabin.

They were coming.

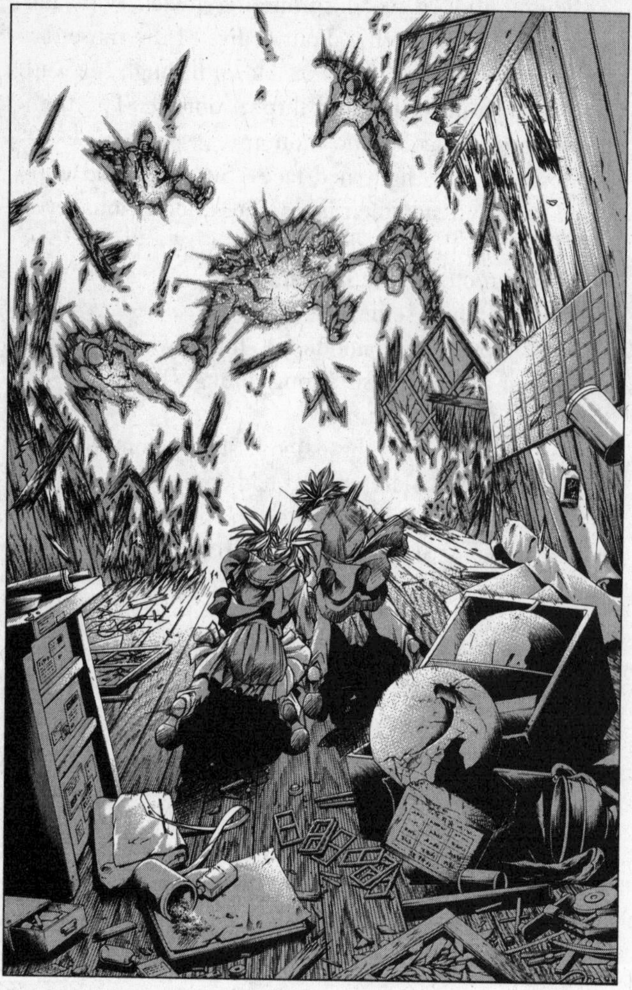

Riot police were coming to kill me.

To kill the monster psychic with their pistols.

Inside my head I was beyond panic, everything went white.

"This way!" Sayaka yelled, beckoning through one of the holes that had been blown through the wall.

"Let's get out of here, Kakeru! The two of us!"

All I could do was follow that voice.

CHAPTER 5

THE CURTAIN RISES ON COMBAT

"Here they come!" Jôi called out in an unusually strong voice.

"Above you, Kaito! Sho Amamiya is heading right for you!" Before Jôi had finished speaking, Sho appeared from the "subspace" right above Kaito's head.

"Drop dead!" Sho took a swing down at Kaito's head with a wooden kendo sword.

But Kaito had an advantage: he had been alerted to the attack just a moment before, thanks to Jôi. He launched his own ambush, firing his pyrokinetic power at Sho.

Whoosh!

It was some explosion.

Kaito's skills had improved rapidly just in the last month. His body wrapped in gigantic flames, he fended off Sho's attack. Sho dodged the flames by teleporting once again.

Then he reappeared thirty feet farther up in the sky, looking down at Kaito and his friends with an arrogant smile. "You've arrived on Avenue One in hell. Anyone who doesn't want to die needs to leave."

"This is it! Everybody scatter! This is where the bloodshed starts!" said Jôi as he began to run.

"Jôi, wait!" Ayano and Xiao Long went after him.

To the two of them running beside him, Jôi said, "Xiao Long, you look for Kakeru with me. Make your power useful by following any of his chi lingering on the street."

"Leave it to me! I remember the 'scent' of Kakeru's chi. I'll be sure to find it!"

Jôi gave a nod of assent. "And Ayano, you go off somewhere and project out of your body. I have a favor to ask of you."

"Anything! What do I need to do?"

"I want you to call for backup."

"Backup?"

"Yes. I'll tell you who and where he will come from. He's the only one who can help Kakeru. That's what my second sight is telling me."

Sho stayed motionless as he looked down on Kaito and Hiyama. That arrogant smile made Hiyama shiver. This was the second time she had seen Sho's power. And even Hiyama, who had no psychic powers, could see that Sho's power had grown. She could feel the psychic energy surging out of him. "Kaito, are you going to be okay by yourself?" Hiyama shouted as she pointed her paralyzer gun at Sho, trying to hold him off.

"Clear out, Hiyama-san! That monster can teleport! That gun's not gonna help. You're just gonna hold me back if you stick around!"

"Fine with me! Okay, it's all yours!" Hiyama ran after Jôi and the others.

"Well, want to go at it man to man, Sho?" Kaito looked up into the evening sky.

Kaito teleported repeatedly, always remaining thirty feet up in the sky.

"Heh heh heh! Pretty full of yourself, aren't you, Kaito?"

"Hah. Now I'm on a totally different level from you. If you don't want to die, you'd better disappear," said Kaito, facing Sho up in the sky. He was proud to back up his tough talk by unleashing his pyrokinetic power. Crimson flames, a few thousand degrees hot, enveloped his body. "Stay away, Sho, unless you wanna get burned."

But Sho still was bursting with confidence. "Hah, you think it's just you that's gotten better, Kaito? I'm warning you. I'm not the same person I was a month ago. My power has increased so much I can hardly believe it myself. Thanks to this drug."

Sho took a tablet out of his pocket, popped it into his mouth and chewed on it. "This, for example!"

It happened in the blink of an eye.

Sho disappeared from the sky, and almost at the same time a huge block of water appeared over Kaito's head.

Sho had brought a large amount of water from someplace. Before, Sho had only been able to instantaneously teleport things he could touch, but now his power had increased to where he could teleport objects he couldn't hold in his hands, like water.

Moreover, tens of tons of it at a time.

"What?!"

Kaito froze in shock. Sho looked down on him. "Cool down that hot head of yours, Fireball," he said.

The block of water opened and spread like the palm of a hand and rushed toward Kaito from a hundred feet above.

Kaito stood dumbfounded. There was no place to run. In one second, the place would be underwater. And taking a direct hit would be incredibly damaging. Water moving at that speed would knock him unconscious— no, it could even claim his life.

"I win." Sho was sure of his victory. But then . . .

Boom!

The sound of an explosion. Everything in front of him went white. It was the kind of water vapor explosion that occurs when water is evaporated in a fraction of a second by thousands of degrees of heat.

"Uwaaaaaa!" Sho was hit with hyperheated steam. He had no time to teleport before he was enveloped by the explosion. At this rate, he would hit the ground.

Desperately, Sho tried to teleport using his last remaining bit of consciousness. But it was too late; Sho fell. Staying up in the sky where Kaito's flames could not reach would be the death of Sho.

It was no use.

He was going to die.

Steam clouded his eyes as he saw the puddle on the ground grow bigger and bigger. *So that is where I'm going to die.*

But just as this thought occurred to him, there was another water vapor explosion from the pool of water. The force of the wind pressure broke Sho's fall. Sho hit the ground and passed out.

Yet the impact was not hard enough to kill him. Kaito had created another blast of water vapor to cushion Sho's fall. Hands in pockets, Kaito strolled over to where Sho lay. The ground around him had been dried completely by the extreme heat.

"I wasn't going to let you die, Sho."

Kaito lent his shoulder to the still unconscious Sho and propped him up. "It's absurd for us psychics to kill

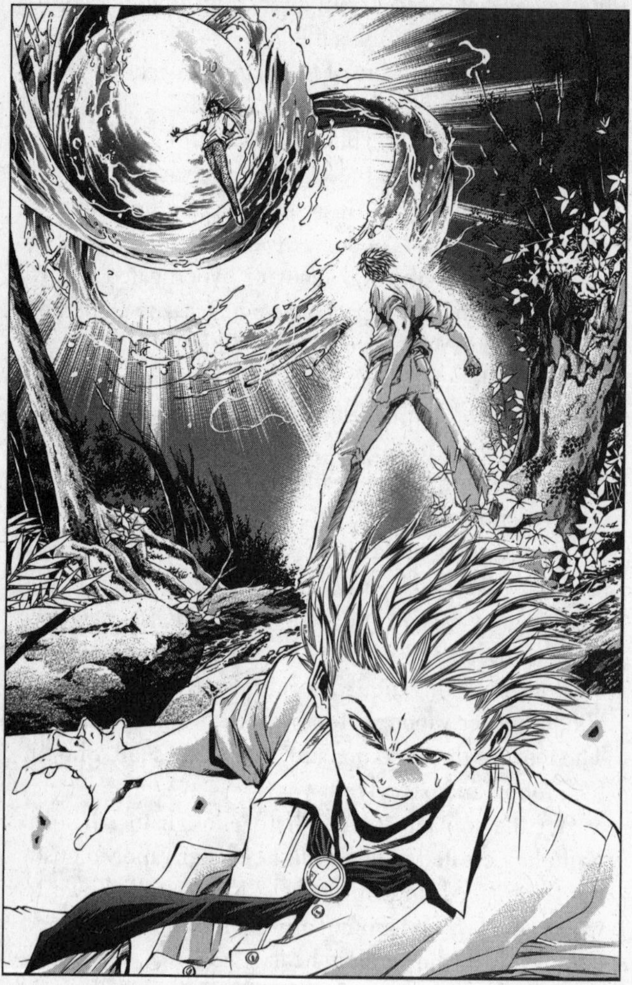

each other. Right?" Kaito went off after his friends, his arms around Sho.

"You don't mind, do you, Jôi?" Kaito murmured in Jôi's general direction. He might be watching with his second sight.

I ran, totally out of breath.

It was my first time running through a forest with no trails. Bamboo leaves cut my hands. I almost twisted my ankle jumping over a fallen tree. But I couldn't just stand still.

Because the police were after me. What if they pointed their guns at me again?

I might use my psychokinesis once more. And, once more, I might kill someone without meaning to.

As I ran, I couldn't stop thinking about it. What happened to those riot police back there? Broken down cabin though it was, they'd been thrown through the wall and then outside. There was no way they weren't hurt. And maybe one of them had even died.

What was I gonna do now? Even if I turned myself in, my power might, on its own . . . no, I could deal with that. But even scarier things might be going on.

Oh, heck yeah. Just maybe, what about something like this? What if I had a split personality, like on these TV shows Sayaka was talking about? What if the other one of me thought nothing of using psychokinesis to kill people, or that girl at the police station who died when her head exploded, maybe I . . .

"It's okay, Kakeru, it doesn't look like they're coming after us." Sayaka grabbed me from behind, almost knocking me over.

Oh, right. She was still with me. I turned back to look for signs in the distance but saw no trace of our pursuers. The sun was about to set, and maybe that terrible accident back there had frightened them into retreating.

Sayaka and I sat down together on a fallen tree. Breathing heavily, I said, "You should go home," and buried my face between my knees.

I was completely exhausted. Why did this have to happen?

Looking back on it, it had all started the night Ayano had come into my room. Since then, everything had changed. Up till now, I'd interpreted this change as for the better, but boy, was I wrong. Who would've known it would come to this?

I was pierced by feelings of deep disgust. I didn't want to kill anyone, and I might have killed a few people back there. It made me want to die here, cowering just like this, miserable and alone.

"Get out of here. Go home."

"I won't. How can you throw me away like this?" Sayaka asked.

"Why is that? Look at what just happened. What if I'm a horrible monster?"

Oh, heck yeah. If I was a nut case, then . . .

"What if I suddenly flip out? I might kill you. You've got to get out of here quick. It's the best thing for . . ."

"No!" Sayaka clung to me. "I've finally met someone like me! I want to be with you. Take me with you, *please*!"

"S-someone like you?" I was confused. What was she saying?

Sh-she couldn't mean . . .

"Are you a psychic, too?"

"Um hm. Not as amazing as you are, of course. I can do about this much," Sayaka said, and shut her eyes.

And then all the squirrels and rabbits that had been

hiding in the forest crept out and gathered around Sayaka, albeit warily. A flapping of wings came from the sky, and birds alighted on her shoulders and knees.

"You have the power to make animals come to you?"

"Yes. Aren't they adorable? And I can talk to them, too."

"Wow. How 'bout that. Gee, um, that's a neat power to have."

"You think so? Thanks." Sayaka said, playing with the animals.

"Hey, you think there's a country where there are only people who have powers like you and me? I sure wish there was. Because then we wouldn't have to hide our powers, and if someone else found out about them it would be okay. And people wouldn't come after us with guns like they did just now."

"Yeah." I remembered Takemaru saying that, too. Suddenly I thought of the Greenhouse.

Back when I thought I wasn't a psychic, I'd thought the Greenhouse was just a terrible place where a group of people were engaged in an insidious plot. Takemaru had said the same thing Sayaka did. But now I saw it from their side. Going to a normal school, surrounded by normal people, made me feel uneasy.

What if I was found out? I'd much rather go to a group that could make use of my powers, and be among my comrades, than have to live with that kind of dread.

Wait! I shook my head. *What on earth was I thinking?! Think about why Ayano and the others ran away from the Greenhouse.*

They told me, didn't they. That it was like a prison. This happening to me might even be a plot by the Farmers at the Greenhouse, for crissakes!

Right, it had to be.

Didn't I already have four good friends who had

powers like mine? No, if you included Takemaru and Sayaka Mamidori, whom I'd also promised to be friends with, then I had six comrades with psychic powers.

Oh, right! I almost forgot. I should tell Sayaka about Ayano and the others. Her feelings of isolation would be much easier to bear if I did, wouldn't they?

"Hey, Sayaka, you know, actually, Jôi, Ayano, and the others are the same as you and I . . ." I said, but Sayaka was distracted. She was looking off in the distance. As if she was frightened of something.

"Sayaka, what's wrong?"

"The animals are afraid of something."

"Huh?"

Suddenly I noticed that the animals were all on guard and looking in the same direction. What could possibly be over there?

Just as I thought that, it happened.

Bang!

A gun fired in the distance.

"Ah!" Sayaka gave a slight moan. She staggered, then crumpled.

"Sayaka? What's wrong? Did something—" Something warm and sticky was on the hand I'd put out to help her. Even though it was very dark, I could tell what it was.

Blood.

Sayaka had been shot.

Most likely by the police!

Blood rushed to my head. "Those bastards!" In my anger I lost control. And then, as if they were in tune with my exploding emotions, the trees in the forest began to creak. I glared in the direction of the gunshot.

"You're not going to get away with this!" Maybe I gave off power fueled by this rage or something, because the trees standing in the direction of my gaze were flattened as if by an unseen bulldozer.

"Uwah!" came a scream from the darkness.

No doubt some riot policeman hidden there had been pinned underneath the fallen trees in the forest.

But this time I wasn't freaked out. My power didn't scare me anymore.

In fact, it was pleasant. It felt like finishing off an enemy in a TV game.

"Ooh . . . wha-what happened?" Sayaka rose, holding her shoulder. Good. The wound was shallow.

"Does it hurt, Sayaka?" I helped her up by her uninjured arm.

"Um hm. It hurts a little. Was I shot?"

"Looks like it. I won't let them get away with this, you have nothing to do with this! Damn it!"

"We have to get away from here, but where can we go?"

"It's okay. There's a place where only people who have powers like us live. According to what Ayano and the others told me, it's a few miles into the forest."

"You're kidding. What's it called?"

After a long pause I said, "The Greenhouse." Sayaka and I walked deeper into the forest.

As we walked, I prayed silently in my heart.

There are psychics there, aren't there? At the Greenhouse.

If there are, if you're watching us from somewhere, please show us how to find you.

I'll become one of you—

Hiyama, Jôi, and Xiao Long entered the forest that Kakeru had run into.

Ayano had already hidden and projected herself, per Jôi's instructions. According to Jôi's second sight, Kakeru was in this forest about half a mile away.

Even though they understood this much, they couldn't move. Jôi and Xiao Long both felt that overwhelming danger awaited them up ahead.

"What are you saying is up ahead?" said Hiyama, exasperated. "Didn't you say that Kakeru's ass is on the line if we don't do something fast? If you're not going, I'll go by myself."

"Wait, Hiyama-san. If we don't proceed in the proper way, then . . ."

Pushing past the stationary Jôi, Hiyama parted the waist-high grass and started into the forest. But then her legs were seized by something strong and powerful.

"What the . . ." Hiyama looked down toward the ground; as accustomed to danger as she was, she let out a shriek. "Aagh! What *is* that?!"

A number of decaying human hands thrust out of the grass, grasping her legs.

"Let go, Leggo—!" Panicking, she tried to shake them off.

But the grotesque hands would not be shaken off. As soon as she shook one off, another would take its place, just like an illusion.

"Jôi! Help, save me . . ." She turned around, but could not see Jôi or Xiao Long. Instead she saw countless armor-clad warriors, shimmering through a haze of heat. Deserted even by the power to scream, she struggled not to faint.

Even as she almost collapsed, she felt a warm hand on her shoulder. Particles of light streamed into her body from the palm of the hand, washing away the fear crawling up from her feet like repulsive insects. The feeling of light all around her allowed Hiyama to return to herself.

The hand on her shoulder was Xiao Long's. "Hiyama-san, are you all right? This is what we meant, that it was dangerous to proceed unprepared."

"Huff, huff, huff . . ." Hiyama panted. "What was that thing just now?" She became aware she was on her knees on the road, a few feet from the grass she had gone through.

"A bazillion decayed hands reached out from the grass. I looked back, but you guys weren't there. Then there were all these warriors in armor . . ."

The cold chill returned; she started to shake, in spite of herself.

"Like evil spirits. Were they an illusion? Was that a nightmare someone used telepathy or something to show me?"

"If that was all it was, we wouldn't be this wary," said Xiao Long.

"What? Well, then you can't mean that was . . ."

"Hiyama-san, what you really saw were evil demons," said Jôi as, pulling her arm, he helped her up. "Well, no, that's not really right. They were wrought by a certain type of psychic. The ability to commune with spirits, or, put simply, a psychic medium. There must be a psychic close by who can use that power."

"I doubt it's anything so simple," said Xiao Long as he himself walked toward the "forest of evil spirits."

"It's a power that molds the spite of those who died here into the demons that Hiyama-san saw. I bet in olden times this was a battlefield. The warriors in armor probably died in battle. That really was a close call. If things had gone badly, you might have been possessed by a spirit and gone insane or had your body taken over and been forced to kill yourself.

Hiyama had no words.

"Stay back, Hiyama-san. They're here again. This time in greater number."

A moan, like a rumble from the earth, resounded deep in the forest. Gradually the number of moans increased, before long bringing with them phantasms shining with pale light. They swayed toward Xiao Long.

How dare you kill us . . .

We curse you and your children, and their children, and theirs . . .

Ohhh . . . ohh . . . ohhh . . .

Even in killing you we will not be satisfied . . .

The blade of malice will tear you apart . . .

The phantasms all mumbled hideous curses as they pressed nearer. A coldness drifted out of the forest to chill the spine as if the temperature in the area had dropped more than twenty degrees. Hiyama felt her skin prickle all over. "Xiao Long! Stop, what are you trying to do?!" she shouted without meaning to.

"Don't worry. Leave this to Xiao Long. Let's go on," said Jôi, as he stood before Hiyama.

"Go on? How?! The forest's a den of evil spirits!"

"Xiao Long will make a space for us. We'll run straight into the forest while he does."

"I can't do that. For me, it's just not possible!"

"It'll be all right. Hold on to me, Hiyama-san. Don't be afraid and believe in yourself. Loosen your feelings and become possessed. Tell yourself you are Akira Hiyama and push aside the spirits that try to come in."

"Telling me that doesn't mean I can do it."

She couldn't stop shaking.

But Kakeru was waiting, she reflected, and did as Jôi said.

"Oh, to hell with it. Who's afraid of a bunch of restless spirits of the dead, anyway?"

At this show of bravado, Jôi squeezed her hand and got himself ready for what was to come. "Xiao Long, we leave it up to you!"

"I know. If I'm not afraid, then I'll have no problems with these guys." Warm yellow light lodged in Xiao Long's outthrust palms.

In the twinkling of an eye, this warm-colored aura spread out over Xiao Long's entire body and draped around him like a robe of light.

"W-wow . . . that light. What is it?" asked Hiyama as she clung to Jôi's arm.

"It's Xiao Long's aura. Auras with good intentions are warm colors, ones with evil intentions are cold colors, and it's largely recognized that anger is reddish, or so I'm told."

Amazed that Jôi could speak so calmly at a time like this, Hiyama asked, "Jôi, are you sure you're in junior high?"

"I mentioned that, didn't I? That if you don't treat me like a kid then I'll go bad."

"Sheesh." Giving a wry smile, she gave Jôi's hand a squeeze.

"Please don't worry. I will protect you, Hiyama-san."

"Okay."

Already the area around the three of them was covered with ghosts.

Curses and a nauseating smell of rot filled the air. So much ill intention and hatred eddied about that an average person would likely have not been able to stay in their right mind.

Warriors brandished rusty swords above their heads in their rotted hands. Thick dark blood flowed from their mouths each time they spit forth their words of malediction. Countless maggots crawled out of the tree-like hollows where their eyes had once been.

"It . . . it's no use. I can't take this even if you tell me not to be afraid." Hiyama clung desperately to Jôi's arm, her heart nearly devoured by fear.

"Xiao Long!"

Jôi's cry was the signal.

The aura enveloping Xiao Long's body turned into fine particles that swirled about, then scattered around the surrounding area just like little particles of fire. As each particle of light struck the "body" of an evil spirit, the curses turned to shrieks, and a hole pierced through the surrounding malice.

"Now!" Still holding Hiyama's hand, Jôi began to run.

Dodging the swords of the oncoming warriors, they wove in and out through the trees.

Don't stop! Run! Don't be afraid! Hiyama told herself as she ran with single-minded devotion.

"Do not look back! Keep your eyes forward!" said Jôi.

"What about Xiao Long?!"

"It's okay. He's strong! He's not going to let a user of evil spirits beat him!"

The two ran, all the while feeling the evil spirits grasping at their backs. They felt one pursuer fall away, and then another. Still they ran on. After a time, they found themselves merely in a dim forest. Xiao Long stood still at the entrance to the forest. He had emitted every bit of aura he had and his body was as heavy as lead. But if he had tried to subdue as many spirits even a month ago he was sure it would not have been possible.

Since he had fled the Greenhouse with Jôi and the others, he had definitely grown and progressed. He didn't know why that was. If there was anyone who knew, it was Jôi. There were many times when even

Xiao Long didn't understand what Jôi was thinking. He was hiding something. There were many things he didn't tell them. Xiao Long was not so insensitive that he did not notice this. Just where was Jôi taking them, anyway? If they went there, could they be happy? Sometimes Xiao Long felt uneasy about this.

Nevertheless, he didn't feel that trusting Jôi and escaping from the Greenhouse had been a mistake. Staying there and having been included in Udoh Karaki, director of the Greenhouse, and Arata Ikushima's foul plot was wrong—of that he was certain.

Suddenly, he felt a presence approaching from deeper in the forest, where the evil spirits disappeared. Resisting his state of lethargy, he raised his face.

It was a girl.

She was older than Xiao Long. Her pale face was expressionless as a Noh mask.

"That was amazing, Xiao Long. You made all of those evil spirits disappear," said the girl, without changing expression.

"Fuyuko . . . Isshiki? That was you manipulating the spirits of the dead just now, wasn't it?"

Fuyuko Isshiki was a spiritualist, the only psychic medium at the Greenhouse.

Her inexplicable power to control spirits was a unique deviation that mystified even the Farmers.

"It's been a month since I last saw you at the Greenhouse, hasn't it, Fuyuko. You haven't changed a bit."

Fuyuko smiled with only her mouth. "I've been seeing you the whole time."

"What?"

"I've been at the same junior high school as you. We saw each other many times and you never noticed?"

"Excuse me?" Xiao Long was stunned.

He was vaguely aware that Jun Todoroki, who stood

out particularly among the students who had transferred to Kikyo ga Oka Junior High at the same time as they had, must have been a psychic sent by the Greenhouse.

But he had felt all the while that Jun Todoroki wasn't the only one.

Xiao Long and the others had escaped from the Greenhouse one month before. At that time, except for a small group, he had known all the psychics in there. They all lived together in the small concrete box that was the Greenhouse, so it was common to see one another.

For this reason, Xiao Long had always thought he would know if one of the students who had transferred in was a psychic from the Greenhouse.

But it seemed he had been naive. There *had* been psychics. He just hadn't noticed them. Why?

Jôi must have noticed them. Why hadn't he told them?

Struggling with the distrust welling up inside of him, he pointed his palms at his foe before him, ready to wring out the last bit of power he had left.

"Uh-oh," Fuyuko drew back. "The battle's over. There's no vengeful spirit around here for me to borrow strength from, and you don't have much aura left, do you? Wouldn't it be life threatening for you to do any more?

"See? Look. Shall we call it a draw, then? Today at least." And turning on her heels, Fuyuko walked back into the forest. "We'll meet again some day, Xiao Long Baim . . ." As she left, her form disappearing into the darkness, Xiao Long dropped to his knees, his strength spent.

"Let's rest a bit, Jôi. I'm at my limit. Even just for a minute," said Hiyama, leaning her back against a standing tree, shoulders heaving violently. Hiyama had trained her body, but the psychological exhaustion was more than she could stand. It made her body feel like lead.

"I'd like to, but it looks like there's a welcoming party."

"Huh?" Hiyama lifted her head and searched the pitch-black forest with her flashlight. "It doesn't look like there's anybody out there."

"You have your paralyzer gun ready, right?"

"Are there Farmers here?"

"Eight of them. And one psychic. It's okay, the two of us can handle this many."

She felt relief at his words. "It's your prescience that tells you that. Right, Jôi?"

"It's just my gut feeling. I told you I didn't know everything, didn't I?"

"Great, *now* you tell me."

Bang, bang bang!

Suddenly there was the sharp sound of impact. Shots from a paralyzer gun.

"Tch." Hiyama dodged as a reflex. "They've got to be pretty far away. Their aim's good, seeing as how dark the forest is."

"That means they've got a psychic with them who has second sight, like I do. This one's probably told them our position."

"The same as you? You can't mean he or she is prescient?"

"This one is not," Jôi said distinctly. Holding his breath and being perfectly still, he looked for signs in the forest.

"I think he's someone I know. He's a powerful psychometer, but he's not prescient. It's all right, he's not my enemy. Get your paralyzer ready. Two Farmers are hiding over in the shadow of that thicket on the right."

"I'm on it!" Hiyama approached the thicket floating in the moonlight, holding the paralyzer in both hands. "Where should I set my sights? Right or left?"

"Two feet to the right. There's another one meter to the right . . . no, make that two and a half."

She fired exactly as directed.

"Oof."

There was a soft groan and the sound of somebody falling.

"Good! Got 'em both!"

"There's another thirty degrees to the left."

Quickly she moved the muzzle, but a shot from in front of them came first.

"Tch!"

The bullet swerved and hit the tree behind. At the same time, she shot. There was another groan. It was in response.

"Three down. What's next?"

"Make a pretty good team, don't we?"

"Be serious. Quick, tell me what's next," she said as she changed the cartridge.

The paralyzer, a powerful stun gun she'd obtained from a captured Farmer, had served her well in the past but had the limitation of only being able to fire three shots before needing a reload.

During the time Hiyama was changing the cartridge, Jôi leaped from the shadow of the trees. He faced his enemy and charged at him like a stray dog.

"Jôi!"

"Cover me!" said Jôi, pushing forward without hesitation.

Bang, bang, bang!

Sharp explosions rang out in the darkness. Several stun guns had been shot point-blank at Jôi as he rushed in to attack. But none found their mark.

As always, Jôi dodged the bullets with small movements, rushed at his hidden enemies like a beast, and felled them all with a single blow.

Hiyama jumped out from the thicket to cover Jôi. One by one she took aim with her stun gun at the Farmers who broke ranks, and put them to sleep with precision.

Although not even a minute had passed, all eight Farmers that Jôi had said were there had been subdued.

"Looks like it's all finished, eh, Jôi?"

Putting out his arm to keep Hiyama from getting any closer, Jôi said, "Not yet. There's still one left. The psychic . . ."

"True to your reputation, Jôi." A slight boy, about the same age as Xiao Long, appeared from behind a large tree. His condescending smile belied his years, although perhaps it was just an effect of the light from the flashlight.

"Toya Akatsuki. I knew it was you," said Jôi as he approached him. "Oops," said Toya as he drew back. "I'm not going to fight. Not with you." Jôi shortened the distance between them.

"Too late to say that now. The reason you've been waiting in ambush is to fight, isn't it? Am I right?"

"Don't be silly. An opponent like you would be no match for me."

"Humph. You mean you're scared?"

"It's not that. I never did want to fight you. I was waiting for the right time, after the Farmers were taken care of. I wanted to talk to you."

Toya took a pistol from his belt and aimed it at Jôi.

Jôi didn't seem at all frightened. "Why'd you do that?" he said, moving another step closer. "You do at least know that something like that won't work on me, don't you?"

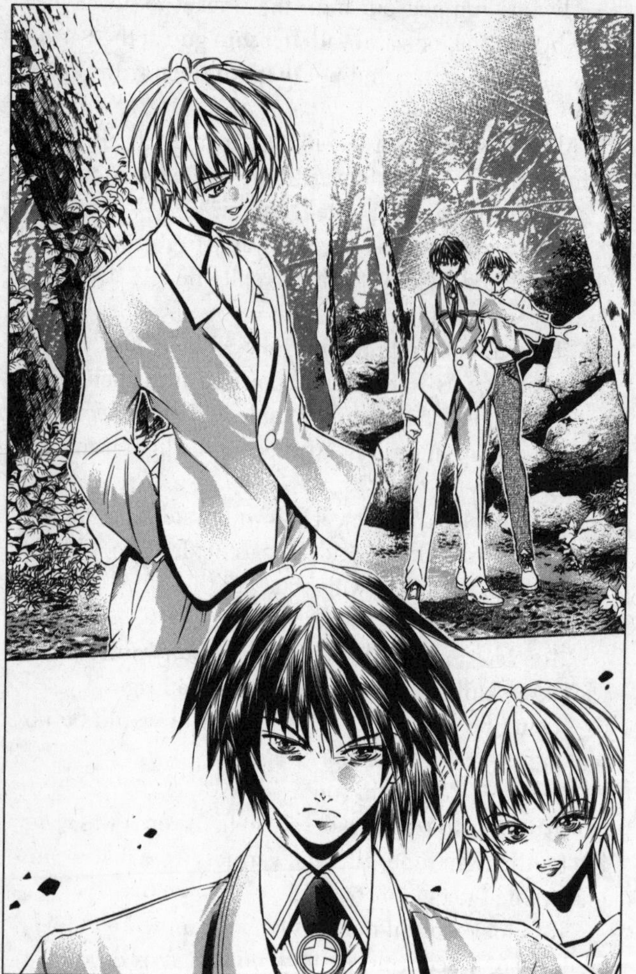

"Granted. But what if I do this?"

He turned the muzzle on Hiyama. "She's just an ordinary person. She can't do tricks like dodging bullets from a pistol. I'm warning you, this is not a stun gun. It's a real pistol that I stole from the armory at the Greenhouse."

"Why, you . . ." Jôi halted. "What do you have to say? I'll listen, but you'd better disappear quick when you're finished."

Toya chuckled. "I can read what other people are thinking, the same as you. The Farmers, Director Karaki, and not even Ikushima know I have read their minds, but I hear it all, every bit. So I know all about you having prescience. Of course, Ikushima did try to hide it."

"Big deal. What's your point?"

"So, I've got a business deal you might like."

"Business deal?"

"I'll tell you what Ikushima is after. In exchange, you'll have to tell me about something, too."

"About *what*?"

"About Category Zero."

Jôi was silent.

"A 'Category Zero'? What's that?" Hiyama asked Jôi.

Jôi said nothing. His face was full of unease that Hiyama had never seen before.

"Come on, Jôi, tell me. What's going to happen if the Category Zero wakes up and figures out what he is? You know, I know you do. If you're planning on using him to your advantage, how about counting me in?"

"Get out of here," Jôi said, taking another step toward Toya.

"Hey, wait. Let's be friends. We have similar powers. We're both nuisances who learn about stuff we'd rather not know. Don't you think that if we worked together, we'd be invincible?"

"Get out of here." An angry aura surged out of Jôi's entire body. Even though Hiyama had no psychic powers, she could feel it clearly.

"W-wait, are you sure you'd rather I shoot? I'm going to shoot her . . . Hey . . . You . . ."

Toya started to point the gun at Hiyama. Hiyama dodged with lightning speed and took aim to return fire with the paralyzer.

"Get shot by a kid like you? You gotta be kidding."

"Get out of here!" Jôi roared angrily.

Toya went rigid. Still pointing the gun, Toya stood frozen, as if he'd been turned to stone.

Hands outstretched, palms down, Jôi approached Toya. Each time he took a step, the weeds thrusting boldly up from the ground withered as if to avoid physical contact.

A feeling of foreboding tightened in Hiyama's chest. "Stop! Jôi!" the words were torn from her throat.

The timing was such that it wasn't clear if Jôi's hands had touched Toya or not.

Jôi was clothed in an aura that blazed like flame. Suddenly he relaxed, as if he'd torn off his armor. Jôi took one of the hands he'd stopped and touched it softly to Toya's cheek. The rigidity simultaneously left Toya's body, and he collapsed, eyes closed as if asleep.

"Jôi, what did you do to him?"

Smiling angelically at Hiyama, who had rushed over to him, he said, "It's okay. He's no longer a psychic. I wouldn't be surprised if he's lost some of his memory, but physically, he's fine."

"What do you mean? Just what *are* you?"

"I can't explain yet. Cut me a little slack, Hiyama-san."

Hiyama considered it all carefully, what he'd done, what he'd said, and that expression she hadn't seen on his face up till now. She meditated on this for an instant and then said, "All right. I won't ask you anything. And I won't tell anybody, either. That's what you want, right, Jôi?"

"Yes. Thanks." Jôi dropped his eyes, gave a little bow with his head, and set off walking into the forest. "Shall we go? If we don't hurry, we'll be too late."

"Yeah." Too late for what? Hiyama nearly asked, but swallowed her words.

In any case, she was sure he would just say he couldn't answer yet. Still, just now, Hiyama had learned something that even Kaito and the others didn't know. The fact that he was not merely clairvoyant.

The Son of God. The words suddenly came to mind.

Yet this boy who would go anywhere and do anything for his comrades looked just like any other ordinary kid. Except there was something in his eyes much older than his fourteen years . . .

She made up the ground between them and asked, "What will happen if we're too late?"

"All I can say now is that *if nothing changes* someone will die. It is already a future that cannot be avoided," Jôi said. He didn't look back.

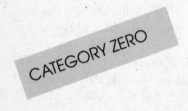
CATEGORY ZERO

Sayaka and I headed for the center of the forest. What with one thing and another, we'd probably already walked a mile or two. The Greenhouse was supposed to be about six miles away from the city. Sayaka and I were still in our school uniforms; we had left our bags at the cabin.

I had no map, of course. Once Ayano had shown me the Greenhouse's location on a map, but without a compass, I couldn't tell what direction was the right one. Nevertheless, we kept on walking, weaving through trees and pushing our way through thickets.

We had a good reason to keep moving. If I really did have psychic powers, the Greenhouse Farmers would come and get us once we got close enough. They had machines, called "Seekers," that detected psychics' unique brain waves. And with so many psychics in the Greenhouse, there had to be one with telepathy who would respond to my call. Walking through the forest I called out to someone, anyone, inside my head: *Kakeru Hase is here. I'm a psychic. If you can hear me, please come. Anybody . . .*

"Um, where is it, this 'Greenhouse'? Do you think we're on the right path?" Sayaka asked uneasily.

"Yeah. I think so. My friends ran away from there, jumped in a river and ended up at that dilapidated cabin we were at, so I thought I'd start by looking for the river."

"A river? Could that be what that noise is?"

"Huh?"

When I stopped and listened carefully, I could hear the sound of running water.

"Why, it's so close! Well, okay, let's go in the direction of the sound of the water. After that we'll head upstream on the bank."

"'Kay."

"How's where you got hurt back there?"

"It seems all right. The bleeding has stopped."

"Then you were probably just grazed. I'm so glad . . ."

"Thank you, Kakeru."

"We'll get you some first aid as soon as we get there."

"'Kay."

Heading toward the sound of water, I found that the river was closer than I'd thought.

"Are you thirsty? It looks like we could drink that water," I said.

Sayaka looked at the river. "You're right. But it's in a gorge, and getting down there looks pretty tough."

"No worries. If you hold on to me . . ." and taking Sayaka's hand, I started to lead her down the steep slope.

The damp earth was slippery, but fortunately I was wearing sneakers. The part where we could hold on to trees probably wouldn't be *that* dangerous. But then, just as I was thinking this—

"Ahh!" Sayaka slipped and fell on her backside.

Holding hands, she pulled me and I stumbled. The two of us tumbled down the steep slope and were thrown onto the riverbank.

"Owwww. Sayaka, are you okay? I'm sorry, I should have kept my mouth shut."

"Ooh, yeah, I'm fine. I think I sprained my ankle."

"Really? All right, then I'll carry you piggyback."

"What?"

"It's all right. Once I carried someone way heavier than you on my back. It was Jôi, from the class next to ours."

"Huh? You carried Jôi piggyback?"

"Um hm. It was hard, too, he's heavy. Compared to him you are next to nothing," and I stooped and proffered my back.

"Well, if it's really okay . . ." Embarrassed, Sayaka climbed on my back.

I headed upstream along the river with her on my back.

"Um, Kakeru?" came Sayaka's voice from my back.

"Hm? What is it?"

"You're psychokinetic, so why are you carrying me on your back?"

"Huh? What do you mean, 'why'? I mean, I don't know how to use it yet. After I get good at using it, I wonder, will I be able to fly?"

"I think maybe so. You should give it a try."

"Oh, no, that's okay. I'll walk."

"But it's hard, isn't it, carrying me. I'm pretty sure you can fly. Why not try to?"

"You may very well be right, but I want to walk while I can."

"Why?"

"Because walking is normal. It's more human to walk, even if you *can* fly. Don't you agree?"

"You're kinda unusual, Kakeru."

I laughed. "You think so? I think I'm pretty normal."

"Can I ask you another question?"

"Sure. What?"

"What do you think you'd like to use your power for?"

"By power, you mean psychokinesis?"

"Uh huh."

"Let me think. If I can, I want to do something to help people."

"By people, do you mean strangers?"

"Yep. My dad told me this once upon a time. He said whether it's money or power, if you have more than other people, doing something for those who have less is as natural as water flowing from a high place to a low place.

Sayaka was quiet.

"So that's why I always thought that if I turned out to be the kind of person who could do something that other people couldn't, I'd do something for the world around me."

"For . . . the world around you?"

"And yet I . . ." Suddenly the things I'd been dealing with welled up inside and I got all choked up. I hunkered down, let Sayaka off, and let out a sob.

"I . . . wanted to help people . . . and I may have ended up killing some . . ."

"Kakeru . . ."

On a sudden impulse, I put my fingers to my mouth. I bit my fingers to try to fight back the tears and keep from crying.

Then it happened.

Strange, how come I don't taste anything? I'm sure that a little bit ago I was . . .

What is this strange feeling of unease? I finally

began to harbor doubt about what I'd been believing. It only triggered an alarm. But that feeling of alarm made all the things I'd felt uneasy about, but just glossed over, come to my mind, as if I were doing a video search or fingering a strand of Buddhist prayer beads.

On one string.

The incident that had thrust me into hell—the girl who had died at the police station when her head exploded. My name had been the last thing she said before she died. Yet the girl's corpse had vanished without a trace. The detective who, right before my very eyes, had been thrown by some unseen force and died.

And then running . . .

People being flung through the air as if in concord with my wrath, the wall being blown out, the trees being mown down . . .

I realized there was an explanation.

I realized . . .

The tension went out of my shoulders, and I became still. I began to chuckle. "Hu hu, hu hu hu . . ."

"What's wrong, Kakeru? Why are you laughing all of a sudden?"

"Ah ha . . . ah ha ha ha . . ."

"Come on, what's wrong?"

"Nothing. Not a thing. Oh man, so *that's* what's going on . . . Ah ha ha . . ."

"Kakeru? Are you all right?" Sayaka peered down at me where I crouched.

"Did you think I'd gone crazy?"

"No, I didn't, but . . ."

"Actually, I figured out something terrible."

"Something terrible?"

"Yep. Y'know, I'm not a psychic after all."

"Huh?"

"Of course, I haven't killed anyone by using psychokinesis. Every bit of that was an illusion that some-one was making me see."

"You can't mean that! How can that be? I mean, I saw it all, too! That detective flying through the air, the trees getting flattened . . ."

"You getting shot in the arm?"

"But the police did that."

"No, they didn't. It's the same thing. All of it, every-thing I saw, every single solitary thing was an illusion shown to me by a psychic. Yes, it was all stuff you made up and put inside my head with telepathy, Sayaka Mamidori, every bit of it!"

For an instant Sayaka looked shocked at my words, but then, quickly, with a pitying look said, "Kakeru, what are you saying? I knew it, you've gone crazy. You poor thing," but I wasn't going to be caught up in that anymore.

"You had me completely taken in. That girl who died at the police station when her head exploded was an illusion you showed to Mr. Kamichika, too, wasn't it? That's why the body disappeared into thin air. The whole thing never happened. It was all your telepathy."

"W-wait just a minute, why would I do a thing like that? It's true that I have psychic powers, but only the power to call out to animals . . ."

"That was just an act, too. To get me to let my guard down. When I think about it really carefully, your be-havior was full of things that were contrived. Like when you showed up suddenly at the library and the first thing you said when you saw me was that you wanted to walk home together. No, even before that, you took a prac-tice swing at getting your hooks in me when you acted like you 'liked' me. Me, who you'd barely even spoken to. That wasn't natural at all. It's not like I'm that popu-lar a guy. Even I know that."

Somehow what I was saying turned kind of masochistic. But now that I thought about it, that had been making me feel uncomfortable from the beginning. But thinking about it, that had been the first time something had not felt right.

Of course, for someone like me who had never had a girlfriend, I had interpreted it in a way that would be good for me.

"You carefully observed my behavior patterns for the last month. Undoubtedly you noticed my habit of calling my house before I go home from school then, too. But I'm always with Ayano. My turn to do library duty came up, and you targeted the time when she and I wouldn't be doing things together and set your trap."

"A trap? I would never do anything like that . . ."

"You can't play innocent with me anymore. I called home, just as you had calculated I would. And my sister asked me something really strange. She asked me if I'd done something the police would want to talk to me about, or something. It didn't occur to me that it was foreshadowing for the illusion of me having psychokinesis you would show me later."

Sayaka glared at me in silence. Probably trying to think up an explanation. "I don't know where fact stopped and illusion started, but I'm guessing that the detectives waiting for me was 'reality.' Which means that Mr. Kamichika's saying the girl's body disappeared after her head exploded at the police station should have tipped me off, and you didn't need to tell me about it. Am I right, Sayaka?"

"I don't have the slightest idea what you're talking about."

"Playing innocent again, aren't you? When I think back, everything you said and did is full of inconsistencies. At first your reason for coming with me was because 'every day was tedious,' or something like that. So then that guy was killed right in front of us. I thought it was pretty weird that you'd run away with someone who might be the one who did it, just because you were bored. And when I said I was going to the police after all, you panicked and stopped me."

Sayaka said nothing.

"But then the riot police stormed the cabin—I'm sure by then it was one of your illusions—and the wall got blown out with a big bang. As might be expected, you couldn't use a reason like 'curiosity' to explain, so you said you were psychic. Well, up to then it was a pretty good story, but having yourself get shot was not a good idea."

"Not a good idea? Why?" Her intonation was different. She sounded resigned.

"Your ulterior motive was to get me angry about you getting shot when you hadn't done anything wrong, so you could show me another illusion of psychokinesis. I felt sticky blood on my hand then. Of course, the blood was an illusion, too. But it made me angry, and when the trees were flattened and I heard the cop's scream, I ran, pulling you with me. I was totally fooled at the time. I'd talked myself into thinking that I was a crazy psychic who had done terrible things unknowingly, in a fury. However, I put my hand to my mouth. I bit my fingers. But there was no smell of blood at all, and no taste of blood either."

Sayaka, annoyed, knit her brow and clicked her tongue.

"You see it, too, don't you. That's why. Your blood was on my right hand and I didn't wipe it off or wash it off. Blood has a strong smell and taste, so I should have smelled it right away when my hand was near my nose, or tasted it when I licked it. You were careless. You forgot to send me the illusion of the smell and taste of blood. And here everything else but that had been perfect. Naturally you didn't take into consideration that I might put my fingers in my mouth."

"Humph. You're a lot smarter than you look. Eh, 'Wild Type'?" Sayaka's voice changed.

Her voice plainly had become that of another person, one whose voice I had heard before.

"So it's you after all, Maya." As I pronounced her name, the false self she had showed me via telepathy dissipated.

The form of Sayaka Mamidori twisted and distorted, and was reconstructed as if molding another figure out of clay. In just an instant, her appearance changed completely. The hint of brown in her hair (of course, it could be that it was dark and I couldn't really tell) became jet black. The wide, beautiful eyes turned to long, sharp slits.

It was Maya, a telepathic psychic from the Greenhouse who I'd fought with one month ago.

"Whew, what a load off my back. I feel refreshed." Maya seemed just as she had before. Crossing her arms impertinently, she said, "It was a lot of work. Really. I had to display the form of Sayaka Mamidori to everyone in class; and to make matters worse, Ayano and the others knew the other four psychics under cover at the junior high school by sight except for one. Making them look like other people kept me really busy. Quite honestly, don't you think I'm the only psychic you'd find if you looked the whole world over that could have pulled it off?"

As she talked on and on, bragging about things I hadn't asked about, Maya was totally unlike Sayaka Mamidori, who was thought of as not just the prettiest

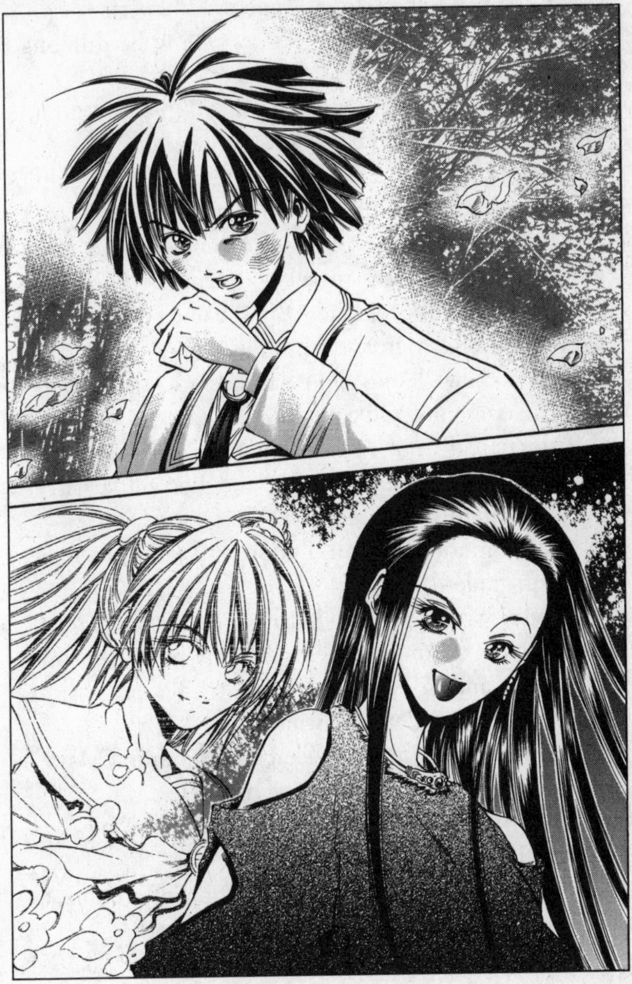

girl in school, but the nicest. Basically, Maya was insufferably full of herself. I should mention, though, that she had a pretty face; it just wasn't at all to my taste.

Well, I was right before; Ayano was the best.

Uh oh, not good. This was no time to be thinking about that.

"Yeah, well, whatever. But what I really want to know is why do this to me? Give me a reason."

One month before I'd been in a battle that I didn't know if I'd survive, but now, for some reason, I wasn't afraid of her. At most, I could only think of her as some girl with attitude from my class. Was it because we'd spent so much time together? But the one I'd spent time with was Sayaka Mamidori, her illusion.

"Who knows? I only did what Ikushima said to do."

"Oh, come on! You can tell me!"

"You're really not a psychokineticist? You made that car crash when we were fighting, and then at the gym at the junior high school . . ."

"No, I'm not one at all. I'm no psychic, just a regular ninth grader."

"You're wrong. I mean, Ikushima said you're a really rare psychic, a Category Zero, like that might show up every thousand years or so."

"Beg pardon? Category what?"

"Don't go blabbing out what you shouldn't, Maya," a young man's voice came out of nowhere.

"Wh-who's there?!" I looked around. My body was floating in midair.

"Whoa! Oh, man! Crap!" I flapped around in midair, but my body only went higher.

"H-help!" After I rose thirty feet in the air like I'd been snagged by a crane, I found the owner of the "power" who had been reeling me in from midair waiting there.

He floated there in midair, hands thrust in his pockets.

"T-Todoroki?

"Don't act all buddy-buddy with me, jerk." Even in the dark, both eyes gave off a bizarre light. Jun Todoroki, the new kid at the school everyone was talking about, who had taken over all the groups of punks in just one month, was a psychic.

"You're Kakeru? Some little no account dude like you is a Category Zero? Who would've believed it?" Our eyes met.

A shiver went down my spine.

He should have been about fourteen, the same as me. But he could have been ten years older. The intensity in his low, whispered voice made my hair stand on end.

This slender boy overflowed with aura too overwhelming for words. A monster. That's the only way I could put it.

I had encountered people who possessed freakish power before, but as we faced each other I had a feeling Todoroki was in a completely different league—truly a psychic monster.

I shrank as if my soul had been pulled from me. He came slowly toward me in midair, hands thrust in his pockets. I couldn't avert my gaze from his cold eyes.

"I was really close to you all this time, you know? I was told to follow Maya's telepathy."

Could it be that the wall of the cabin blowing out and the trees being flattened were not telepathically induced illusions?

Come to think about it, Maya and I *had* walked out through the hole in the cabin . . .

Which meant that his psychokinesis had the destructive force of a bulldozer, a crane, or dynamite.

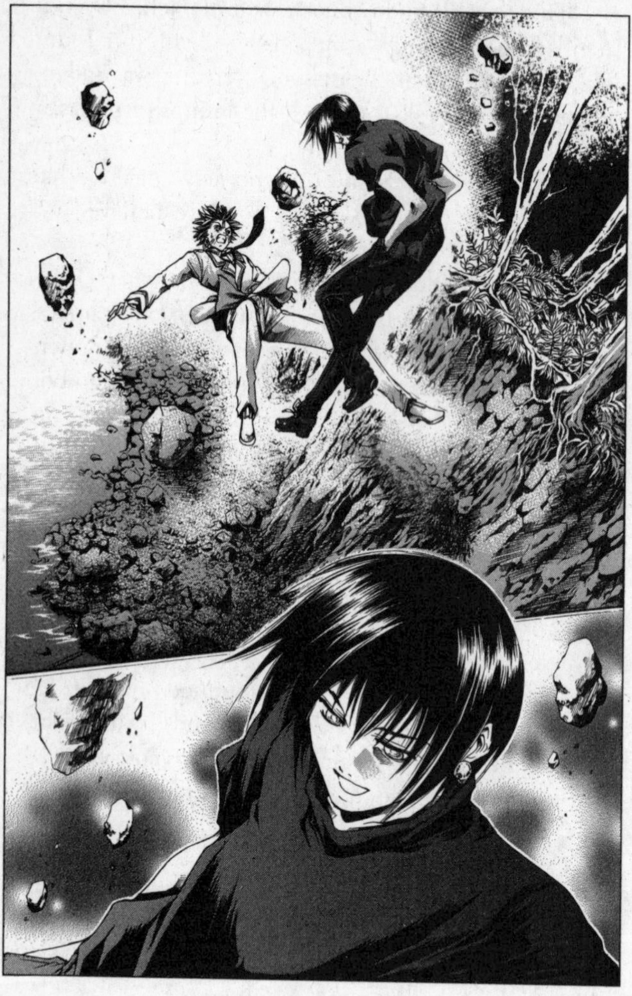

Killing me would be as easy as trampling a tiny ant with your foot.

"On top of everything, look at you! You're not worth my time."

Jun Todoroki's shining eyes had now approached to a couple feet in front of me.

I couldn't even yelp. He was going to kill me. Somebody save me.

"Stop, Todoroki!"

Todoroki stopped looking straight at me and cast his eyes down below. His power on me eased and I descended as if I was going down in a high-speed elevator. I picked up acceleration and smashed against the ground.

"Uwa!" The shock was at least as great as if I'd jumped off a second-floor balcony. If I'd fallen on concrete, I might have been seriously injured.

I got up, rubbing my backside where I'd landed. Maya stood in front of me, as if to shield me. "You can't kill him," she said to him as he came down to a height of just a few feet off the ground. "Ikushima told you to bring him to the Greenhouse, didn't he? If you do anything else, you'll be disobeying orders."

Had she tried to save me?

Nah, why would she do that? Most likely just following this guy Ikushima's orders.

"Ikushima? Ha!" Todoroki gave a scornful laugh.

"I'm warning you, unlike you 'Cultivated' psychics, I am not controlled by strange medicine. The only reason I did what Ikushima asked and came here is because I was interested in the Category Zero. That's all."

"That's what I mean. The Category Zero you're interested in, it's *him*! If you kill him because the strategy failed, we'll lose it all! So let's just take him to the Greenhouse. We'll get there as fast as flying on a jet plane if you use your power. Yeah, we should have done this first thing. It would have been so much easier if we had used your psychokinesis or Sho's power to teleport to take us. This trying to get him to want to go to the Greenhouse on his own has really dragged on and on."

Th-that would be bad. I wasn't even close to being psychic, and me going there wasn't going to do anything. And what was a "Category Zero"? I'd heard that psychics like Ayano who could use their power at will were called Category Ones, but . . .

Was "Zero" higher than "One"?

Couldn't be.

No way could something like that happen.

"Humph. You don't get it, do you," said Jun Todoroki. "Well, not surprising, I guess. I'm the only one he told what the real meaning of Category Zero is, after all."

At his words, Maya stopped. "I beg your pardon? What does *that* mean? What is the real meaning of Category Zero? What do you mean, it's something just between you and Mr. Ikushima?"

"You don't need to know. Because this is a 'contract' between me and Ikushima. You third-rate psychics have never been part of it."

Gaping in surprise, I watched them take shots at each other like they were in a Ping-Pong match. Such internal discord all of a sudden? What the heck was that about?

"What are you trying to do, Todoroki? What did Mr. Ikushima tell you to do?"

"I *told* you, you don't need to know."

Again, Todoroki's eyes began to shine with a pale light in the darkness, and I knew he was getting ready to use his power again. His eyes gleamed like a cat's in the dark right before he used his power. If that was the only thing I'd seen, I'd still think there was something seriously different about him from the other psychics I knew.

It wasn't only that he was a powerful psychic; the feeling he gave me was fiendish, sinister.

"Hey, come on, stop. Don't kill him. Please." Maya stepped between Todoroki and me.

"He's not such a bad guy. What I mean is, he really is a nice guy. I feel like we need him at the Greenhouse. So . . ."

Again she came to my defense. She might not be so bad after all.

"Humph. This is too funny. You in love with him, Maya?"

"Huh?! What are you saying?! Of course not! It's just that I . . ."

N-no way . . .

Cuz when we were running all around, I'd been thinking what a nice person she was, but those were my feelings for Sayaka Mamidori.

"Don't get the wrong idea!" Maya said to me, her cheeks flushed. Petrified, she gave me a kick.

Ow. Damn it, no I was right before, she was awful.

"You're the one who has the wrong idea, Maya," said Todoroki.

His eyes glowed brighter and brighter, and his body started to be enveloped in his pale aura.

"I have no intention of killing him. What Ikushima told me to do if this plan failed was to kill someone right in front of the Category Zero."

"S-someone?" Maya asked in return, backing away.

"There's no one else here but you." Maya was blown over backward before he finished.

"Kya—!" she screamed as she struck the rocks on the riverbank. "What are . . ." she choked. Maya coughed violently as she crouched. She'd been struck hard on the back and was unable to breathe. The way things looked, she wasn't going to be able to use telepathy.

"Well, what's wrong? How about using that telepathy you're so proud of to put up a fight?"

Maya floated gently, spinning as she bounced off the ground, rocks, and trees like a pachinko ball.

"H-help . . . hel—"

Uh oh.

At this rate, she really was going to be killed! On the other hand, what could I do? Oh, damn. I cursed my own powerlessness. Category Zero. Big deal. If there's anything I can do, somebody tell me!

"Come on, will you hurry up and die already?"

Maya was thrown into the river and didn't come up. Oh, what was I going to do? At this rate, she would drown. I had to save her.

"Yo, Todoroki!" I finally managed to speak.

"Yeah? What is it, Category Zero?"

"Why are you doing this right in front of me? If you're trying to threaten me with this to get me to go to the Greenhouse, then it's not going to . . ."

"You're all talk and no action."

"Huh?"

"Look at me. Do you think logic is going to work?"

I was silent.

N-now that he mentioned it, what could I do besides use logic?

There was a cough and a gasp. "Save me, Kakeru!" Maya popped her head out from the river and looked at me, her face contorted.

"Please . . . save me . . ."

"It's no use. This guy's a coward," said Todoroki coldly, shifting his eyes to over her head.

Squelch, rattle rattle . . .

There was a sound like something from a construction site. A gigantic rock weighing several tons was dragged into midair from the cliff directly above Maya.

"Save me, Kakeru . . ."

"Die." With that one word from Todoroki, the rock fell toward Maya like an invisible wire had been cut.

Ker-unch.

There was a sickening sound. Maya could no longer be seen in the river.

"No way . . ."

I trembled.

"No way . . ."

My heart trembled.

Why hadn't I gone to save her?

I was . . .

A coward. Just as Todoroki had said. The worst of cowards.

I felt something explode inside my head.

Like the explosion of a star, it turned into brilliant particles of light, covering first the inside of my head before blotting out everything around me.

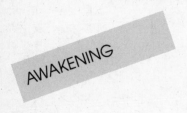

CHAPTER 7

AWAKENING

After the sound of the explosion, I saw:

"Kya—!" Maya screamed, striking the stones in the riverbed.

"Wh-what are . . . cough . . ." she coughed violently as she was swirled about.

She'd been struck hard on the back and was unable to breathe. The way things looked, she wasn't going to be able to use telepathy.

"Well, what's wrong? How about using that telepathy you're so proud of to put up a fight?"

Maya floated gently, spinning as she bounced off the ground, rocks, and trees like a pachinko ball.

"H-help . . . hel . . ."

Uh oh. At this rate, she really was going to be killed! On the other hand, what could I do? Oh, damn. I cursed my own powerlessness. Category Zero. Big deal. If there's anything I can do, somebody tell me!

"Come on, will you hurry up and die already?"

Maya crashed into the river and didn't come up. Oh,

what was I going to do? At this rate, she would drown. I had to save her . . .

"Maya!" I broke into a run and jumped into the river, aiming for the spot where Maya had gone under. I put my arms out wide to look for her in the pitch-black river.

My hands touched something soft.

Frantically, I pulled her up.

Maya's face broke out of the water and she clung to me.

Choking, she said, "K-Kakeru, uh . . . I . . ."

"It's okay. You leave this to me!" I was saying stuff I knew I could not back up. I really was just a little bluffer.

She coughed again. "Please, Todoroki . . . get rid of him . . ."

She pulled herself up on the shore and lost consciousness.

"Hu-ff hu-ff hu-ff," I breathed, shoulders heaving, as I glared at Todoroki.

You're over the line, buddy!

To do something like that to a girl, and one of your comrades, to boot!

"Yo, Todoroki!"

"Yeah? What is it, Category Zero?"

"Why are you doing this right in front of me? If you're trying to threaten me with this to get me to go to the Greenhouse, it's not going to—"

"That is not my intention."

"Huh?"

"I'm just doing what I was told to do. I was told to kill someone in front of you, so I'm just going to kill her."

"You're crazy. Definitely insane."

"Get out of my way, Category Zero. You want to get killed, too?" Todoroki said coldly, his gaze shifting to above my head.

I followed his gaze up to see an enormous rock that stuck out from the cliff, creaking ominously.

"You don't mean . . . !" He was going to crush us with that rock?!

Squelch, clatter clatter . . .

The rock came away from the cliff and hung suspended in midair, as if dangling from a crane. The boulder must have weighed several tons. If that thing fell down on us, we'd be squashed flat.

"Stop!" Desperately, I dragged Maya so as to avoid the rock when it fell.

"It's no use. If you want to live, you either have to abandon her or give me a performance in a way that only a Category Zero can."

"You've got it all wrong! I'm no psychic!"

"Oh yeah? Then I don't need you. You can die together." The boulder lurched in midair, then started to fall.

This was it.

We were going to die.

Squashed flat, right here.

Then, just at the moment I had prepared myself for it, it happened.

Boom!

The boulder was smashed into pieces in the air a few feet above our heads. Just like it had been blown up by some kind of explosive.

For a second I seriously thought that was what had happened. But if so, the blast would have gotten us, too.

But not one piece of stone came down on us. It was almost as if we were protected by an unseen umbrella.

"Tch . . ." Todoroki clucked his tongue in irritation. Todoroki took his hands out of his pockets. Alighting on the ground, he came toward me.

"Category Zero, did *you* do that?"

No, I was pretty sure I hadn't. I started thinking maybe I . . .

"It looks like I made it in time, eh, Kakeru?" came a voice I'd heard before.

Hey, right! That was . . .

"Takemaru?"

I looked up. He appeared out of the full moon. He landed gracefully on the ground, stood before me, and extended his hands.

"Can you stand?"

"Um hm."

I grasped the hand and he pulled me up. He was fourteen, and although small for his age, the hand he extended told me he was filled to the brim with confidence.

Takemaru. A psychokineticist. Another one of my valuable friends.

"Did you explode that rock?"

"Yeah."

"Wow. Your power is a few times stronger, no, hundreds of times more powerful than before."

"I told you, right? In a letter. Every day since you saved me, my power has gotten stronger. So much it even scares me. So that's why"—Takemaru glared at Todoroki—"someone like him's not going to beat me. I'm going to rip him apart in no time at all."

"Humph. So you're that turncoat psychokineticist? Maybe you can use psychokinesis a little bit, but after all, you are Cultivated, aren't you. Do you really think you can beat a Wild Type like me?"

Todoroki's eyes started to glow and out of nowhere, there was a resounding rumble from the ground. The trees rustled, and countless pebbles and large stones started to make sounds as they struck each other. Even I

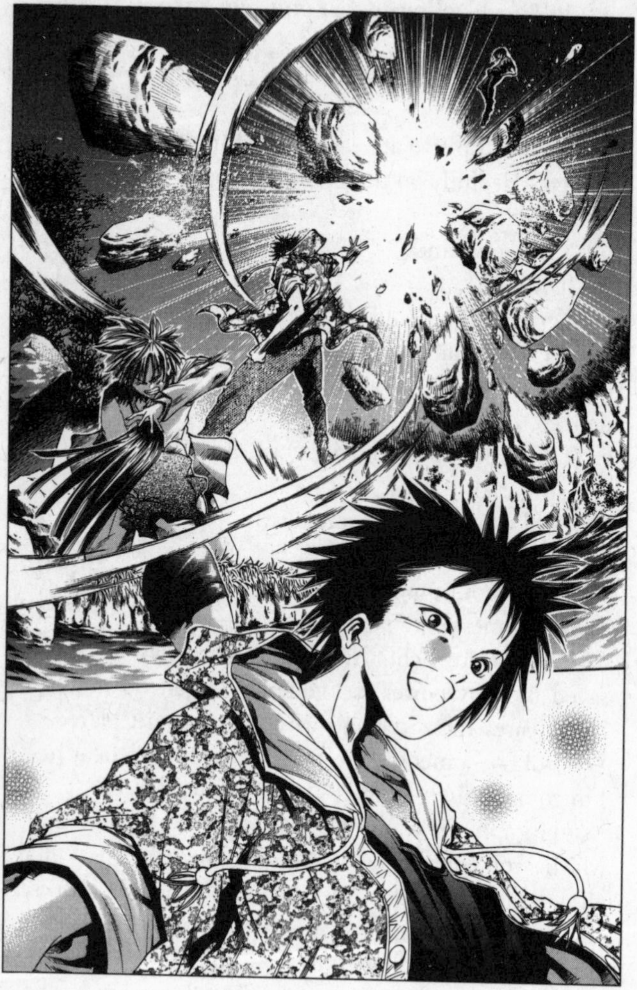

could feel the fierce storm of psychic waves raging around us.

"Try it and see!" said Takemaru, holding his own with Todoroki.

He stood in an easy stance with no tension. Just seeing that, I understood the true meaning of how he had grown. This whole time he had been in a special hospital, and I had only spoken with him via the letters we exchanged.

So it had been one month since we'd met like this. Somehow I was really happy to see him. And hopeful.

When Takemaru concentrated his powers, the rumbling from the earth and the noise from the trees stopped, and the rocks and stones settled down.

"Well, well. You do some interesting stuff. You offset my psychic waves by hitting them with your own pulses in opposite phases. That's an advanced technique. I wouldn't have thought you were a Cultivated psychic."

Todoroki's face was confident as he said this. He might not have showed us what he could *really* do yet. In that case, how was this battle going to turn out? If the two of them really went at it for real, just being close by might be risky.

"You should put some space between you and us, Kakeru. Because it might get pretty messed up around here," said Takemaru.

"Uh, yeah, all right," I said, hoisting Maya onto my back.

"No need to run away, Kakeru" came another voice I'd heard before. Or rather, a voice I heard all the time.

"Jôi! I knew you'd come!" Tears came to my eyes at the sight of him sprinting down the slope toward the mountain stream.

"We've come to rescue you, Kakeru." Hiyama-san was with him.

"Kakeru!"

"You're all right?"

Even Xiao Long and Kaito were here!

"Uwa!" I let out a scream as I felt something fly inside my head.

"Ayano, you came, too?"

Of course. Sorry to be so late. I went to get Takemaru.

"What? *You* went to get Takemaru?"

"Yeah, she did. What a shock," said Takemaru.

Jôi said I should. He said Takemaru was the only one who could save you.

Now we were all here.

"Yo, you're Todoroki, aren't you. Whatcha gonna do? You want to take all of us on?" said Kaito, stepping forward.

"No," said Todoroki. Well, of course. Who'd be able to defeat this many psychic opponents no matter what an incomparable monster he was.

"I wouldn't mind killing all of you right here and now, but it would do more harm than good. My 'job' is done. I'll cut you a break today." At the moment he said that, he disappeared into the darkness, leaving behind a gust of wind.

"He teleported? You mean that jerk wasn't a psychokineticist?" said Kaito.

Jôi looked up at the sky. "That *was* psychokinesis. It looked like he disappeared because he instantaneously accelerated to his top speed of several hundred miles per hour."

"Wha . . . Seriously?"

"Yep. He's not just talking big. He really is confident that he can take all of us on at once."

"That guy . . . Holy Jumping Jesus!"

He said his job here was done . . . said Ayano.

"What job?" I asked Jôi.

Jôi shook his head no, eyes down toward the ground. "I wish I knew. I don't know, either. The 'door' is still locked. But I'm sure this is not over yet."

"Does this mean that someday this may happen again, Jôi?" said Xiao Long, sounding irked. Jôi nodded.

"Probably. And not all that far off."

"Humph. Who cares? Next time when he comes I'm going to tear him limb from limb," said Takemaru. All eyes turned to him.

"Thank you for coming, Takemaru," said Jôi, holding out his right hand. They must have known each other when they were at the Greenhouse, but by no means did it look as if the relationship had been a good one. Ayano had mentioned that apparently Takemaru, who was a Cultivated psychic, had hated Jôi, a Wild Type of psychic who was described as a prodigy.

To think that Takemaru coming at Jôi's urging would be the catalyst for this amazing pair to join hands.

"Humph." Dashing my hopes, Takemaru did not take Jôi's hand and turned away, nose in the air. "Let me tell you something. I didn't come because you and Ayano summoned me, because I don't want to be friends with you one bit."

"Takemaru, don't be that way; you're all psychics, so you should try to get along . . ." but Takemaru interrupted me before I could finish.

"Kakeru. I came for you. Only for you."

"Huh?"

"You are my *friend*. You're the only person in the world I can trust."

"Takemaru . . ." Takemaru's feelings made me happy. Even if this had resulted from him mistakenly thinking I was a psychic and had used my power to save his life.

"Well heck, considering it's you, if you really went after him, you could probably finish him off pretty easily without me. But look, I don't know why, but you almost never use your power, until you're in danger, do you? So I thought maybe there was something I could do."

"Gosh, you really saved me. Thanks, Takemaru."

Takemaru gave an "aw shucks" sort of smile. My chest tightened at Takemaru's words. The only person in the world he could trust. It pained me that Takemaru felt so isolated that he said these words to an outsider like me, and not to his parents.

"Christ, what a loser!" Kaito rudely ran up to Takemaru and punched him in the stomach.

"Ow! What'd you do that for? You want to die?" Takemaru glared at him.

"Hey, you two! Hang on a sec . . ." I tried to get between them. Kaito pushed me back.

"Hey, Takemaru? You make me sick and I *still* can't stand you. But whether or not you can trust someone, is that any reason not to take the hand offered to you in friendship?"

Takemaru did not reply.

"If all you ever do is drive away anyone who tries to get close, you're not ever going to be able to have any real friends. You agree with me, Kakeru, don't you."

"W-well, I um, I mean, uh, Takemaru's my friend . . ."

"Jesus! Take a stand! At a time like this, you have to tell him how it is!"

"But, y'know, Takemaru."

"Huh?"

"You and Jôi are both my friends."

Again, Takemaru said nothing. Takemaru looked confused, and then, with a fierce expression on his face, he approached Jôi.

"Ah, wa-wait, Takemaru . . ." At his expression, I went to stop him.

But there was no need. With that fierce expression, Takemaru faced Jôi and extended his right hand. Despite his amazement, Jôi smiled and firmly grasped the hand he was offered.

I was relieved. "Yo, junior high school student! Don't you think you'd better get along home?" Hiyama put in, flicking me hard on the forehead with her thumb and middle finger.

"Ack, oh no! Oh, right, Takemaru, would you use your telekinesis to take me home? Right away?" I asked Takemaru, putting both my hands together.

"Why don't you fly home yourself?" asked Takemaru.

"Well, I dunno . . . I'm kind of tired . . ." which wasn't really a good excuse, but what more could I say?

"I'm *home!*" I said in the most energetic voice I could manage as I opened the door.

After what had happened on the phone, I figured my mother and sisters would be pretty angry. Actually, I was completely exhausted, but I felt it could be risky if I didn't try to fool them by being energetic, so I did my best to look and sound cheerful.

On the other side of the door were three faces. It looked like they'd been sitting with their legs folded under them, waiting in the hall by the front door for me to come home.

"I'm home," I said again, with a meek look.

"Is that all you've got to say, 'I'm home'?!" my mother shouted first.

"Do you have any idea what time it is? It's one in the morning! Where on earth would a junior high school student have a reason to wander around to until this hour?!"

The sheer force of this knocked me onto my backside before I could step from where I took off my shoes.

"I-I'm sorry . . ." my voice got softer and softer.

"You could have at least called!" This time it was my oldest sister. "Mr. Kamichika—or rather the police, came to our house! We asked him if you'd done something, and he said he'd met up with you at the school gate after class let out."

"Uh, yeah, he did, but I . . ."

"He said when he asked you some questions, you said something incomprehensible and suddenly ran off. What's more, you were holding some girl by the hand. Tell us the truth about what happened. If you don't, we're not going to let you in! Right, Mother?"

So *that* was how it happened.

Everything from that tough-looking cop getting blown away like that and dying had been an illusion that Maya had created telepathically, so to Mr. Kamichika, it must have looked like I said something crazy and suddenly ran off.

"Well, Kakeru? Tell the truth. I won't be angry. Where were you and what did you do?" asked my mom. Her voice suddenly became quiet, but this meant she was *really* angry.

"I'm pretty sure I know what happened," said my middle sister as she nodded repeatedly, in an incomprehensible reaction.

Just what kind of speculation had been flying around while I wasn't here? It scared me just to think about it. But if I told them what had really happened, they'd cart me off to the hospital, and how was I going to explain things?

Oh, right, there was something I had to ask. "I'll answer you. But Suzue, would you tell me something?"

"What?"

"Mr. Kamichika came here before I got home, right?"

"Yes. What about it?"

"Did he say anything? About what happened at the police station?"

"Oh, that. He apologized. He said he had asked you about something incomprehensible that shocked you and you ran off. He said he came to apologize."

"That's all?"

"Um hm, you mean what happened to that girl at the police station? It was all a misunderstanding. The girl's home now."

"Oh, oh really . . ."

"But he swears he really saw it happen right in front of him. His supervisor told him to go to the hospital. Isn't it awful to say something like that?"

"I see . . ."

What a relief. I knew that the girl dying had also been Maya's telepathy, but if the girl had been a real junior high school student, I would have worried a little about where she'd got to.

"So . . . what kind of shape was she in?"

"She'd lost her memory or something like that. But wait a sec, why are you so interested in that? It has nothing to do with you, does it!"

"She's right!" Hanae interrupted.

"Instead you should be fessing up! What were you doing until you got home? I already know! You're covered with mud and your clothes are a wreck! Where were you 'doing it'? The park? Or some deserted farmhouse? There are still some around here, aren't there. I'm right, aren't I?!"

Huh? What did she mean, "doing it"? What a time for her to get the wrong idea.

If I answered yes, then who knew what they'd ask me

and do to me, and if I said no, then what would be an acceptable excuse for everything? Oh, man, this was hard. Somebody save me! Jôi, you know, don't you? What answer would get the best results in a time like this.

I wish you would tell me . . .

"What am I going to do with you?" asked my mother as she sighed once again.

"And just when your father was all set to come back home!" Although she sounded angry, she also sounded like she was hiding how happy she was.

"H-he is?! He's not going to be off working far away anymore?! Yippee! Yippeeee!" I jumped up and did a little dance as I walked up into the house.

"Ah! Hey, I haven't finished lecturing you yet!"

"Kakeru! You have to confess!" My sisters chased me, but I shook them off as I jumped about.

It was half that I was really happy. The rest was me taking advantage of this chance to sweep what had happened tonight under the rug.

After handing Sho Amamiya, Maya Kasuga, and Toya Akatsuki over to staff from Crimers, Jôi and Hiyama separated from Ayano, Kaito, Xiao Long, and Takemaru to head for the janitor's room at Kikyo ga Oka Junior High. Hiyama forced an invitation on Jôi because she had things to ask him.

It was after one in the morning, and Hiyama, who had been busily bustling around since seven that morning, was at the peak of exhaustion. However, if she didn't verify with Jôi the truth of what had happened, there was no way she'd be able to get to sleep.

After serving coffee to Jôi as he sat quietly, Hiyama got right to the point. "Well, Jôi, this time, you're going to tell me for sure. You definitely said to me that at that rate, someone was going to die. That this future was unavoidable. But that was a strange way to put it. If it was an unavoidable future, why did you say 'at this rate'? You said you can't change the future. Which means nothing you do will change things, right? But then why did you use those words?"

"I suppose the excuse that I misspoke wouldn't work on you?" said Jôi. As might be expected, he was so distressed he didn't even reach for his coffee.

"Of course not. If you're not going to tell me, go home. But on the other hand, if you tell me, I swear to God I will not tell anyone else. I promise that."

"All right." Jôi gave a sigh and began to speak.

"Someone was supposed to die. You can depend on that. My prescience picked up the worst-case scenario. But I didn't get an 'image' where I could see it definitely, so I thought there was some possibility it could be avoided and used Ayano to summon Takemaru. But when the psychic Toya Akatsuki showed up, he might have triggered a vision that was more concrete. I saw Maya Kasuga's 'death.' "

"Maya's that girl with the jet black hair? But she didn't die, did she? That means your prediction was off."

"No. That is not what it means."

"But in fact . . ."

"In that vision Maya Kasuga was crushed under a boulder. I have no doubt she died once. That is the one and only answer for the 'unavoidable future.' "

"What do you mean? That . . ."

"If you think of that as a time paradox, it's not impossible. Which means that when the future with the worst-case scenario arrived, someone 'did it over again.' That's the only thing I can think of."

"You mean like playing a game?" Hiyama felt a cold

shiver down her spine. "You can't mean that 'someone' was . . ."

"Kakeru Hase . . . Category Zero. Kakeru's a 'Time Rewinder'—that is to say, he's a psychic with the ability to rewind time."

"I . . . I don't believe it. Kakeru's so carefree, and he's a . . ."

"Kakeru's power has probably manifested itself many times before. He's experienced the worst possible outcome, reflected on it without realizing it, and redone things many, many times. So the miracles that have saved him up till now were not due to psychokinesis. I'm sure they were due to him running through things over and over until that one in a million chance occurred. It's just that he has the ability to reverse time until that fortuity occurred."

"It was necessary for him to repeat things a million times for the one in a million miracle. Is that the theory?"

"Yes. If you want to get a one when you throw dice, you just need to keep throwing them until you get that result. Kakeru can do that. That is a terrifying thing. Next to my prescience, the impact it has is beyond compare."

"That's absurd, but if it's true, then he's . . ."

"I'm pretty sure that meeting us psychics was the impetus that drew that ability out of him. And now Kakeru's . . . his effect as a Category Zero already extends to all psychics who come into contact with him."

"You mean the abilities of all of you progress by leaps and bounds?"

"I think so. Even I can now sometimes see wisps of a 'future that must not be known' that I was never able to see before. It terrifies me." Upset, Jôi frowned and forced down a sip of still-scalding coffee.

As Hiyama watched Jôi, an odd thought came into the corner of her mind.

"Jôi . . . have you ever heard the story of the Hundredth Monkey?"

"Yes. Isn't that the story where the monkeys on one island washed their sweet potatoes before eating them, and after a while monkeys on other islands that had no contact with the first one started to do it, too?"

"Geez, you're pretty knowledgeable, considering you're only in ninth grade. But I bet you don't know this little story about glycerin."

"Glycerin? You mean that gooey liquid stuff?"

"Right. Glycerin crystallizes easily below seventeen degrees Celsius, but a long time ago scholars tried everything they could to get it to do that."

"Did they really?" Jôi answered disinterestedly.

"Then suddenly one day about one hundred years ago, they found some glycerin that had crystallized in a barrel in some freighter ship, without anything being added to it. As a group, the scientists divided up that crystal and used it as the 'seed' to successfully get glycerin to crystallize."

"I guess sometimes things work out like that."

"Yeah. Well, I'm okay with it up to this point. The problem is what happened afterward. While the scholars who got some of the crystals from the barrel were conducting experiments on it, they say all of the glycerin in the laboratory started crystallizing at seventeen degrees Celsius. Even the stuff that was shut in airtight containers. Don't you think this is an odd story? That now glycerin is a liquid that crystallizes easily below seventeen degrees Celsius."

"Hiyama, perhaps Kakeru has become the 'first crystal.' Is that what you want to say?" said Jôi. Disbelief was written all over his face. For him this was a rare thing.

For some reason, whenever Jôi talked about Kakeru, he got a new, strange look on his face.

Feeling a new interest in the relationship between the two, Hiyama said, "I wouldn't go that far. But if, as you say, he is a Time Rewinder, you mustn't let him find out about it. Understand, Jôi?"

"Yes. Of course. For his sake . . . and for mine."

Hiyama felt she could only know half of what Jôi, who wouldn't say all of what was on his mind, meant. But what was the other half? Perhaps the rest lay hidden in the pasts of Kakeru and Jôi that nobody knew.

Someday, I'd like to know. But even as she thought that, there was trepidation in her heart somewhere for the time it would be revealed.

She wouldn't be surprised if that was the time the two young men would have to part.

It was just a feeling she had.

It was decided directly after Todoroki finished his "job" that he would be shut up in the Greenhouse.

This was done at Ikushima's suggestion, because they were about to be stormed by the Crimers. It was widely acknowledged that Director Udoh Karaki's errors had brought on the situation.

This was because Ikushima had maintained before the Masquerade that everything had resulted from Karaki's aggressive methods of acquiring potential psychics. These aggressive methods consisted of establishing an "extracurricular study program" in order to conduct research on people with psychic qualifications in the town where Jôi and the others lived.

Karaki believed that, for some reason, the area was a point of significance where many people with psychic competency could be found. That was why Karaki had pulled so many Farmers from other similar private school prep programs around the country, concentrating the firm's combat resources. Ikushima made the point that the result was clear: seven potential psychics had been found in just one month and brought to the Greenhouse by force. With seven people disappearing from the same area in so short a period, there was an inevitable outcry—one that caused the center to be marked by the police and had invited a criminal investigation.

In the end the center was closed, and six out of the seven potential psychics were returned to their homes, memories erased. And now, even the Greenhouse, the largest laboratory of the underground organization FARM, was in the middle of a withdrawal operation.

Of course, Ikushima acknowledged that this was all happening because of his own plan. There'd been a cold war mentality at the Greenhouse—kill or be killed—owing to the bad feeling between Ikushima and Karaki. Ikushima had decided that victory had come to him because he'd sprung his trap first, and did not feel he'd played dirty. Karaki's record with FARM ensured that he was not expelled from the organization, although he could not avoid being demoted. Ikushima sneered at Karaki, saying that he'd only gotten what he deserved, but he had the feeling that some day Karaki might return. Then it would be payback time.

I've got to hurry up and make my next move. My first move went very well. The next move is already taking shape inside my head . . .

He mused on this as he walked through the now hollow gigantic concrete box. A human shadow stood at the other end of the long hall, hands thrust in pockets.

In a puff of wind, this shadow instantly moved before Ikushima. It looked as if he had used the power of teleportation, but what he had done was a jump of sheer force via brilliant use of psychokinesis.

"Yo, Ikushima. Been a long time since we talked together, hasn't it?"

"Jun Todoroki. Haven't you gotten on the helicopter yet?"

"I'm not getting on any stinkin' helicopter. I can fly on my own."

"I warn you, if you're thinking of running away, you'd better stop. There's a microchip in your head that will instantly destroy your brain at the single touch of a button on my remote control."

"I know, geez. But in addition to that, I'm thinking that now I will go along with your plan, so don't worry."

"I am relieved to hear that."

"It's just as you say. I don't know how or why, but in the end, I failed."

"When you knew the first plan had failed, you did as I told you, which was to kill someone in front of Kakeru Hase, and you tried to carry that out."

"Because we had a bet. If I succeeded, you would have removed the chip from my head. If I failed, I would go along with your plan."

"You said failure was impossible. Obviously. Our computer bank popped out the results that someone with your ability had a chance of failure of less than one in one hundred million. Regardless, you failed to kill Maya. Do you know why?"

"It was because of the Category Zero's power, wasn't it?"

"Right. I know why."

"Tell me."

"You succeeded. However, that 'history' was rewound and erased. Just like a video taken by mistake."

"What do you mean?"

"It is not easy to explain. I will tell you sooner or later. Perhaps at the time the plan starts up."

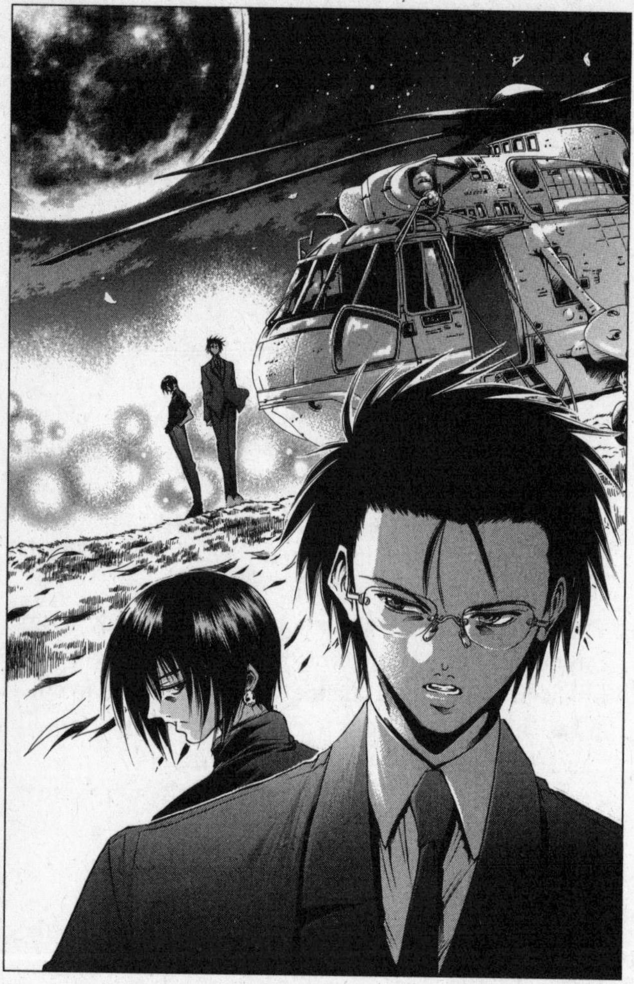

"Humph. Fine. I can wait."

"I warn you, don't think next time is going to go like this time did."

"Yeah? Because there's a Category Zero? Or because of Jôi? You don't mean because of that psychokineticist Takemaru, do you?" Todoroki chuckled.

"That's not what I'm saying. I have received information that someone even more formidable may join in the battle."

"Someone more formidable?"

"Yes."

Ikushima turned his back on Todoroki.

"Ryoma Hase. Category Zero . . . Kakeru Hase's father."

To be continued in *Psycho Busters: Book Three*, the conclusion to the story!

Born in Tokyo in 1962, the versatile *Yuya Aoki* has won acclaim and popularity in Japan for his work in manga, prose fiction, and television. He is best known in the United States for the smash hit manga series *Get Backers*.

Rando Ayamine was born in Japan's Hyogo prefecture in 1974. After graduating from the Tokyo Animation Institute, he became the assistant to Fujisawa Toru, the famed creator of *GTO*. He first headlined his own manga series with *Get Backers*, created in collaboration with Yuya Aoki.